SHE

SHE

FIVE KEYS TO UNLOCK THE POWER OF WOMEN IN MINISTRY

KAROLINE M. LEWIS

Abingdon Press

Nashville

SHE:
FIVE KEYS TO UNLOCK THE POWER OF WOMEN IN MINISTRY

Copyright © 2016 by Abingdon Press

All rights reserved.

This book is printed on acid-free paper.

Library of Congress Cataloging-in-Publication Data

Names: Lewis, Karoline M., 1966- author.
Title: She : five keys to unlock the power of women in ministry / by Karoline
    Lewis.
Description: First [edition]. | Nashville, Tennessee : Abingdon Press, 2016.
    | Includes bibliographical references and index.
Identifiers: LCCN 2016009044 (print) | LCCN 2016009633 (ebook) | ISBN
    9781501804946 (pbk. : alk. paper) | ISBN 9781501804953 (e-book)
Subjects: LCSH: Women in church work. | Women in Christianity.
Classification: LCC BV676 .L49 2016 (print) | LCC BV676 (ebook) | DDC
    253.082—dc23
LC record available at http://lccn.loc.gov/2016009044

16 17 18 19 20 21 22 23 24 25—10 9 8 7 6 5 4 3 2 1
MANUFACTURED IN THE UNITED STATES OF AMERICA

"You are a Jew," she replied, "and I am a Samaritan woman. How can you ask me for a drink of water when Jews and Samaritans won't have anything to do with each other?" The inadequacies we see in ourselves, that we think the world affirms, God sees as extraordinary gifts. God needs us all to make "for God so loved the world" a reality. SHE *gets us closer to that reality.*

CONTENTS

PREFACE

RATHER BY ACCIDENT, one of the classes I started teaching at my current educational institution was Women in Ministry, even though my primary areas of teaching competence are preaching and the New Testament. The person who had regularly taught the course was leaving the seminary, and the general consensus among those around the table planning the class offerings for the following year was that we simply would not offer the course. "Wait a minute!" I said. "We have to offer this course. If no one is willing to teach the course, I will!"

What was I thinking? What did I know about teaching a course called Women in Ministry? Not much, this I knew; but I did know that this course absolutely had to be available to our students. In the few years I had been teaching, I had already had too many conversations with female students about the lack of opportunities in our curriculum for them to learn how to deal with the challenges of doing ministry as women, challenges they were facing in their seminary classrooms from professors and fellow students alike, as well as in their contextual learning sites and in their internships. Furthermore, as a woman in ministry, I had too many friends working in churches and various church settings who were struggling with challenges in their ministry that seemed directly connected to their gender. And I had my own share of issues, both in the parish and in academic settings, which stemmed directly from being a woman in this historically male-dominated field. There was simply no way that I would allow this course to be sidelined in our curriculum.

I could not have predicted how critical this course would end up becoming to the seminary curriculum, to the student community, and to me. It became more and more clear that this course was essential, not only for women entering into ministry but also for the fabric of our educational commitments as a seminary. This course was not merely a place to learn about what it means to be a woman in ministry—it was a space to *feel* what it means to be a woman in ministry. That is, it was a space that insisted on honesty, allowed the experiences of others to be the textbooks for learning, and invited embodiment and self-discovery as subjects worthy of seminary study. As a professor, there is hardly a moment of more profound joy than when pedagogy and formation converge in the classroom.

Over the years that I have been teaching this class, the following list has developed as representative of the primary course objectives:

- To create a safe space for conversation, dialogue, concerns, and questions around women in ministry.
- To acknowledge the sociological, theological, and practical challenges that women face in ministry.
- To connect issues of sexism, sexuality, embodiment, and appropriate boundaries for women in ministry to self-care practices for seminarians and public leaders.
- To explore strategies for successful and authentic leadership.
- To develop a theology of leadership and a leadership development plan that will guide one's ministry.
- To learn practices of accompaniment and regard in mutual ministry settings.
- To grow in biblical understanding of women and leadership.
- To acquire resources for ongoing learning and support as leaders in community.
- To explore one's own sense of embodied ministry and begin to live into that reality.
- To appreciate the many differences in leadership and ministry, and to imagine working relationships that acknowledge the gifts and experiences of all persons.

I share this list now because, in many respects, these are the goals of this book. It is my desire that the reader of this book will not only come away with a better sense of the issues women in ministry face but that the reader of this book will also experience affirmation and an invitation to be able to live fully into the minister—and the person—God has called her to be. As an author, there is a longing for the possibility that what you put down on paper is more than words on a page—that it is an invitation to the reader to imagine, albeit briefly, where change and transformation might happen in her own context.

While this book is meant to be a primer for women in ministry as well as an introduction to and presentation of the issues that women face in ministry, it is also biographical. It is important to acknowledge my own contexts—I am white, heterosexual, and ordained in a mainline denomination, having served in a parish in suburban Atlanta. I am a professor in a seminary representing the same denomination in which I was ordained, the Evangelical Lutheran Church in America. My contexts determine the perspective of this book and how its stories are told. While it is not merely a book of stories about my experiences or the experiences of others, my story and the stories of women I have known—colleagues, friends, classmates, students—are at the heart of this book, and it is written from that viewpoint. What I hope is that this book might accompany you as you live into your own story of who you are as a woman in ministry.

What you will find in this book is a series of chapters that address the FIVE KEYS that I suggest as fundamental to unlocking your power as a woman in ministry. At the same time, I hope you will also be encouraged to discover your own set of keys. For this book to do what I want it to do, it has to be personalized, internalized, and concretized in your own identity as a woman in ministry.

ACKNOWLEDGMENTS

I am especially grateful to Constance Stella at Abingdon Press for her interest in me as an author and particularly for her enthusiasm about, and commitment to, the subject matter of this book. The experience of being a woman in ministry must continue to be a subject of attention in publishing, so that the entirety of the church might live into full expression of God's people.

I am so thankful for dear friends Sonja Hagander, Elisabeth Johnson, Karri Anderson, Sarah Breckinridge Schwartz, Leesa Soderlind, and Caroline Satre, who have been my support group for what it means to be a woman in ministry. We have been talking about these issues for years, since our seminary days, usually over lunch and a lot of wine, and now they are finally in print. For my colleagues Lois Malcolm, Carla Dahl, Theresa Latini, and Amy Marga, who have been my primary conversation partners about what the issues surrounding being a woman in ministry look like in a seminary setting, this book gives voice to our joys and our struggles. And to the wonderful women in ministry I have come to know over the years, especially Eliza Buchakjian-Tweedy, who read through the manuscript and gave critical feedback—a truth-telling experience. She also collected and sent me, with permission to quote them, story after story after story of women who have known and lived the truths named in this book. Behind every story she sent, behind every story that I have been told, behind every story I could tell and have lived are a hundred more, which is why this book and these issues have to be heard.

It is hard to imagine how books get written without the support of family and friends. For my dear friend Gwen Fulsang and her husband, Mike Alexander, who take care of me on my writing retreats, and for my husband, Mark, and my sons, Sig and Stellan, who give me space to write: I am so grateful.

This book would not have been imaginable were it not for the students who have signed up for the course each year and helped me develop the course into what it is now. It is to these students, whom I have had the privilege and honor of accompanying as they embraced their full gifts and power as persons in ministry, that this book, with love and deep affection, is dedicated.

I asked God if it was okay to be melodramatic
     and she said yes
I asked her if it was okay to be short
     and she said it sure is
I asked her if I could wear nail polish
or not wear nail polish
     and she said honey
     she calls me that sometimes
     she said you can do just exactly
     what you want to
Thanks God I said
And is it even okay if I don't paragraph
my letters
     Sweetcakes, God said
who knows where she picked that up
     what I'm telling you is
     Yes Yes Yes
—Kaylin Haught[1]

INTRODUCTION

THIS BOOK IS an exercise in truth-telling and an acknowledgment of what happens when the truth gets told. There is no better encapsulation of truth-telling and women in ministry than the well-known saying popularized by Gloria Steinem, "The truth will set you free, but first it will piss you off." It should come as no surprise that women still face challenges in ministry roles in the church. Yet all too frequently it is indeed a surprise—and not a good one. Rather than being met by a church that is open to and affirming of their call, women going into ministry are confronted by issues that should be over by now. We should know better by now. But we are not and we do not and it is not helpful to anyone—to the women going into ministry or to the church itself—to perpetuate a false perception that we have miraculously managed to move to a church ideal where all who feel called to serve the church are welcome. This ideal was never the case in the early church, not even in its beginnings as an itinerant movement, and it certainly is not the case today.

Nor is it helpful to argue or insist that the church is ontologically different from the rest the world and its potentially corrupt institutions, that the church is an oasis of acceptance and hospitality, or that the church is devoid of humanity's brokenness that leads to power gone awry. The church is not immune to dysfunction, and no amount of belief otherwise will free it from that truth. While we certainly want it to be true that the church *should* be these things, it is not and, in fact, can be far worse than secular institutions. We know this to be true; we have experienced it as true; yet all too often this truth is sidelined so as to make the church look better than it is. Perhaps it is a self-protective mechanism—we need the church to be more than it is because our call is at stake. This is why truth-telling is absolutely essential for unlocking the power of women in ministry, in part because the church itself cannot live into the fullness of the gospel when exclusionary power structures continue to exist.

This book will be about truth-telling on multiple levels. Hiding the truth, or pretending that the truth is not the truth, is not a helpful strategy in general; but in the case of navigating what it looks like to be a woman in ministry, it is a strategy that will only lead to difficulty and even a demoralized sense of the purpose of ministry. Of course, and as we will see as we go along, sometimes we have to withhold the truth because it is not the right thing in that moment. But the sooner the truth about what it means to be a woman in ministry is named and acknowledged, the better women in ministry and those who support them can engage the issues that actually matter when it comes to successful ministry. Yet, as noted above, the truth is often hard to hear. Chances are good that, at first, we will feel more discomfort than comfort or encouragement.

This book has to be about naming, in the words of one woman, "the heartbreak, the scarring of the soul, the weight that is carried in this calling."[2] This book has to be about truth-telling and release: telling the truth of the challenges but also the truth of God's love. It has to be about the release from the weight of carrying it all on your own.

FOCUS AND FRAMING QUESTIONS

There are many approaches that a book like this might take, and other offerings on this subject matter represent that kind of spectrum. A survey of books on women in ministry will include historical accounts; biblical analyses; and autobiographical, anecdotal, and experiential discussions. None of these approaches is better than another—you just have to know what they can and cannot do, as well as the intended purpose of a given volume. However, this book provides a comprehensive taxonomy of issues essential for any woman going into ministry, all in one volume, and with various options, methods, strategies, and approaches for managing the realities of being a woman in ministry.

The intent of this book is to collect these disparate issues into one place for the purpose of providing a comprehensive primer for women going into ministry. The FIVE KEYS presented here are meant to summarize matters pertaining to women in ministry that are currently scattered across various genres. At the same time, this book intends not only to present the issues but to name their motivating causes and offer points of possible negotiation—even hope.

An underlying truth that is helpful to name at the beginning of this book is that the issue is rarely the issue. This is true of life, true of ministry in general, but all the more true when it comes to being a woman in ministry. In other words, questions about the validity of your ministry, your ability to do ministry, or who you are in ministry all have a causal point that has little to do with those specific questions, or is only tangentially related; the stated questions have more to do with unnamed and unexamined assumptions and expectations than the issue named on the surface. Being able to identify this underlying matter when addressing a superficial issue as presented is an important strategy for success. If you spend your time and energy tending the manifesting topic rather than the fundamental concern, this will be a significant cause, at best, for fatigue in your ministry and, at worst, for burnout. Managing the indications without addressing their root cause will also lead to a personal sense of loss—and likely an actual loss—of your own power.

HOPES FOR THE READER

A book like this has some rather lofty hopes for the reader, similar to those that emerge when a group of women gather together. It is in this gathering that we sense commonality, shared experience, support—that we are not alone. That we are not on our own. That we are not just "making stuff up" in our heads, or that we must be wrong. In other words, in picking up this book and reading it, you become a member of this community, the community of women in ministry both past and present. You will find yourself among the cloud of witnesses; you will feel yourself standing on the shoulders of those who have gone before you. This book is not just about you, but about your place in a community that needs to hear your voice. You are entering into your own place of power as well as a space that has its own power as well.

It is essential to note that when we speak of women in ministry we acknowledge that what it means to be a woman is allowed its fullest expression. It is beyond the scope of this book to address the full spectrum of intersectionality with regard to gender binary, the shift in perspective that arises from being lesbian or transgender, and the added prejudices that come with homophobia and transphobia. The perspective of this book is admittedly heterosexual and privileged, as noted in the preface. At the same time, the intent is that the issues presented in this book are shared at some level by all women. Part of our call as women in ministry is to recognize that even these shared experiences, however, are contextualized by the truths of who we are.

This book has in mind women going into various types of ministry in all kinds of settings, not just ordained clergy in traditional parish settings or congregations. Not all women in ministry are called to ministries of word and sacrament. Women in any leadership roles in churches will face similar issues. While there are certainly unique challenges that ordained women face, which will be discussed at various points in this book, one of the prevailing challenges for women in ministry is a rather unhelpful divide between clergy and lay women working in the church. We do not help the situation by maintaining this divide, as if one is better than the other or as if one group really wants to be ordained because "that is what they have been waiting for all these years, they just don't know it yet." There are women in non-ordained positions of leadership in the church, like Associates in Ministry, church staff positions, deaconesses, chaplains, church council presidents, and other paid positions who face, by virtue of gender, the same issues as the ordained.

To perpetuate this divide is also to fuel the fire of women against women. One of the saddest truths about the resistance *to* women in ministry is that it often comes *from* women, and that the most unsupportive group out there when it comes to women in ministry is women themselves. We have experienced this to be true. Why is that? One of the main reasons is unspoken assertions across the board that clergy are better than laypersons, regardless of gender. Women inherit this assumption when they move into ordained ministry. Some of the resistance to women in ministry from other women is certainly lodged in envy, jealousy, and competitiveness. Regardless of whether or not women want to be pastors or leaders in the church, the wariness with which women will approach you has to do with their own desires for meaning in life, purpose, and power. You have a power they want, you are someone they want to be, or you are that which they have not been allowed to be. Knowing this in advance can open up the space for conversation and mutual support rather than backstabbing and suspicion. Some of this tension may present itself as generational, especially if you are a member of a denomination that has started recently ordaining women. At the same time, even young women struggling in their careers will see in you something they wish to be but which they are unable to recognize fully. As a result, an essential premise of this book is the need to support all women as they strive to live into their unique expressions of self in the church, no matter what that calling is.

It is my ultimate hope that this book will someday be outdated. In the meantime, we have to imagine and anticipate these realities for our own immediate purposes but also for those with whom we serve. This book is not just about you but also about those with whom you will do ministry. This means, by extension, that this book is not just for women, but for men, congregations, and places of ministry that are committed to accompanying women in ministry for the sake of reciprocal success and the potential to thrive. It is not enough to change ourselves. We are called to be active in the change of our surroundings. While you have a responsibility to yourself as a woman in ministry, you also have a responsibility to your context of ministry, which will inevitably have questions and concerns about your leadership. This book is about supporting you in your ministry, but also about how you can come alongside the persons to whom you minister and answer questions together. Furthermore, we have the responsibility to help members in our contexts of ministry to be able to have conversations with those outside our communities who question the validity of our leadership. We need to unlock their power for dialogue around theology, ministry, and how God works in the world. We do them no favors by pretending that our ministry is not an issue, because someone will certainly make it an issue for them. We want them to be able to articulate the importance and legitimacy of our ministry without defensiveness, argumentation, coercion, or rejection. They cannot simply be our defenders. Nor should they be in a position where all they can do is remain silent because they do not have the language to talk about leadership in God's church. We are responsible for giving our community members the tools to articulate their own understandings of women in ministry and leadership, particularly in the contexts of their own faith commitments and the places in which they live out their faith and vocations.

This is why truth-telling is so important. Men need to know the truth. Church members and ministry supporters need to know the truth. When the truth is suppressed, when your truth is suppressed, it is then and there that assumptions take over. It is critical to name the truth, to put it out on the table for all to deal with rather than to maintain our current practices of ignorance or pretension. When you are accustomed to hiding the truth and overlooking it, it then becomes almost impossible even to discern truth from falsehood.

The premise of this book as truth-telling also acknowledges that the truth is hard to hear—and will be resisted, sometimes only at first, sometimes perpetually and even exponentially. There will be readers of this book who will think, "That is simply not true. I have never experienced anything like that." But that is when the truth has to be heard for the sake of empowering the other. For there will be those who will hear the truth of this book and say, "You have just told my story. How can I continue?" That is when the truth has to be heard so that you know you are not alone. It is a great time to be a woman in ministry, but it can get better. We just need to know that others think what we think and feel what we feel, so that ministry does not continue as the lonely profession it so often seems to be.

OVERVIEW OF THE STRUCTURE OF THE BOOK AND SUGGESTIONS FOR HOW TO USE IT

Each chapter is devoted to one of the FIVE KEYS. The focus of each chapter, the essential key being described, is clearly stated at the beginning. Truth-telling starts with clarity. If you cannot state the truth with clarity and conviction, it is easy for that truth to get hidden in all kinds of other issues that circle around it and pull attention away from being able to hear the truth in the first place. Each chapter lays out the issues centralized around the key being presented, concludes with exercises and/ or questions for discussion and reflection, and provides a list of resources specific to that topic for further deliberation and study.

First, we might imagine that this book is a necessary read for any woman considering answering the call to ministry. Indeed, this is certainly its primary audience. With this in mind, this book will find an audience in seminary students, which is why exercises and questions are included at the end of each chapter. This book could easily be developed into a syllabus for a course on women in ministry in a classroom setting. The exercises and questions for engaging the primary issues can be answered on one's own or in a group or classroom setting.

Secondly, however, this book is meant to be a resource for any church or ministry setting committed to a representation of the breadth of God's people in its leadership, and not just for the sake of tokenism. If a congregation or ministry setting wants its women in leadership to flourish, these are the five areas of which it has to be aware and to which it must tend. In this regard, parts of chapters could be used for small group ministry, retreats, church councils, and other instances where the goal is to provide ways by which women in ministry are supported—not just to survive but to thrive.

At the same time, this book might find an audience in women who have been in ministry for quite some time, not for the sake of gleaning new information, but for the comfort that indeed they are not alone. It is unfortunately well documented that retention rates of women in ministry are far lower than their male counterparts in the church. Women in ministry need to be reminded that their experiences cannot be personalized and that experiences of sexism are not merely incidences that they have simply "made up" in their heads or that they were being "overly sensitive." Essential to success in ministry is camaraderie and collegiality regardless of gender.

A FEW NOTES ABOUT THE WORD 'POWER'

The title of this book includes the word *power*. As soon as you use the word *power* when it comes to the church, you need to be very clear about what you mean by the word and how you are using it. One way to define power is to consider the preposition attached to it: power "for," "under," "with," or "from." In the case of the title of this book, the rather benign preposition *of* carries a lot of weight. The purpose of this book is for women in ministry to claim the agency of their power. That is, "the power *of* women in ministry" means that women in ministry have power. Period. This power does not need to be enabled, affirmed, or empowered—it just is. The point of this book is not to provide answers for gaining power. It is to acknowledge, to state clearly, that this power is already present. It is to provide ways by which to imagine how that power can be unlocked and exercised not only for the sake of an individual's call to ministry but also for the sake of the community's call to nurture the ministry of all of its members.

Claiming your power as a woman in ministry has to come first from yourself. There will be resistance to this. This resistance resides in an idealism of Christ's power: that we need to have the kind of power that Christ had, the power of emptying himself, power for the sake of the other alone (Phil 2:1-11). Of course, this is a Christian virtue. But you cannot exercise power, even for the sake of the other, if you do not acknowledge that you have power in the first place. You have to be able to articulate where your power is based, but do not let your answers be the lofty ones that you think others want to hear—like your sense of call, your vocation, or your baptismal identity—if those really are not true and if you do not know what any of those claims actually mean. To claim power from within is to be grounded in the absolute truth of who you are. The key before all of these keys is to tell the truth about yourself. If you consistently defer your power externally, the external forces will eventually take over and define your power for you. You will lose your voice.

Power that is acknowledged as coming from the place of truth about one's self is truly the kind of power that makes a difference—and it will save you from those who are intent on taking your power away. This book originates from this personal necessity that true power comes from identity and authenticity. Power is not only something that you *have* but represents who you *are*.

At the same time, the kind of power assumed by and outlined in this book is that which is premised on the true power of God's love to change the world. An ideal claim perhaps, but when the power that we know we have is not grounded in God's power in love, it is easy for any claims about power to become personal or personally driven. What happens when power usurps mercy? When power demands drama? When power manipulates and connives and only looks out for the self? That is power in its most destructive form.

The fact is that the church has a history of power in those destructive forms. The truth is that the church has demonstrated power that has been damaging, demoralizing, debilitating, demeaning, desecrating, and discriminating. And the wielding of the church's power has led to the insistence that some inherently have more of it than others when it comes to doing and being church. Arguments for and against women in ministry are, in part, arguments about power—who can and cannot have it. In the end, for the church to allow women in ministry is a relinquishing of power, and even the church, whose power is nominally based on the Christlike empowerment of others, has had a hard time letting go of control.

Specifically, for the church fully to support women in ministry, it means that the church has to give up the misogynistic practices that have so long undergirded its power: the power to control biblical interpretation, the power to control the image of what a representative of the church should look like, and the power to control, as if one can, human sexuality and gender identity/expression. At the same time, the power of women in ministry can be wielded to empower the church to broaden its understanding and interpretation of the biblical witnesses so as to offer and teach the fullness of God's vision, even to those who are resistant.

Why? Because we all have the potential to dismiss the origin of destructive power, which comes when we lack recognizing our starting point. Where you start determines your end. What controls you? Domination or dignity? Self-service or true service to the other? Self-protection or honor? Self-preservation or pleasing the other? The starting point of your power matters.

If you cannot articulate the seat of your power—that you have it and that you know what to do with it—then your power will have the potential to disempower others, your power will eventually be taken away from you, or the keeping of your power will be your motivating force instead of the power of the gospel. If you do not know the starting place of your power—and whether or not it comes from love, dignity, honor, and glory—then abuse of power and the usurping of it is just around the corner. There is no lack of examples and circumstances in the church where power is yielded with a complete lack of self-awareness. And a letter of call is no justification for yielding unchecked power.

This becomes the litmus test for power. When power's starting point is money, rules, control, competition, manipulation, or the bottom line, then that's not power. That's bullying. That's abuse. That's coercion. That's narcissism. Then what you stand for and what you believe—your thoughts, your ideas, your aspirations, your truth, your sense of justice, your commitment to mercy, and your dedication to preaching the truth of the gospel—is commodified rather than celebrated. We are simultaneously drawn to power and repulsed by it. And that convergence or juxtaposition is at the heart of the issues that surround women in ministry.

God's people have been the recipients of the generosity of power and the objects of the negativity of power. To be a woman in ministry means that you have to come clean about your own power, as well as how you use it and how you think about it. Leadership positions in the church are freighted with an extraordinary amount of unacknowledged, unchecked, and unregulated power. It is critical when entering ministry to reflect on where your power is rooted. Church leaders have the potential to model power that comes from a starting point that is rare in this world: a starting point of truth and mercy, of grace and dignity, of regard and respect. This is the kind of power that will truly save the world.

GOING FORWARD

The process of truth-telling is essential in ministry, regardless of any issue we use to divert the promises of God. When the truth is not told, theology is allowed to spin off into abstraction at best and personalization at worst. Those persons called to and entrusted with the privilege of giving voice to God's love must be held accountable to that which the gospel in its fullness proclaims. This is the essential truth of this book. Women in ministry give witness to the breadth and depth of what we dare to imagine is the potential and possibility of God's grace. When our voices are sidelined, when our presence is questioned, when our presentation of the gospel is called into question, it is never, ever just about us. It is also about the imagination of God. When our imagination for God's hope for the church is undermined by our lack of imagination, that is when God becomes less than God. That is what is at stake for this book.

KEY NUMBER ONE

THE TRUTH ABOUT WOMEN, THE BIBLE, FEMINISM, AND THEOLOGY

Wild

Sometimes it's not so much that I am in the wilderness,
    but that the wilderness is in me. Perhaps for you as well.
Storms stir and waters rise
    and though the wilderness within is drenched, fires burn hot.
For me, this is hell—
    caught somewhere between drowning and going up in flames.
But never forget that you yourself were created wild, which is why you should not fear.
    Never forget that your cry need not be tame.
    And if your voice shakes
I pray you feel no shame because now and then even the earth itself quakes.
But more than that,
    Know that you are not and never will be alone. Know that when you pass through
        the waters you will come out baptized.
    And when you walk through fire
        the phoenix within will be revealed.
Born a new creation
    out of the ashes of resurrection. Still wild, still called by name.
—Annie Langseth (Women in Ministry student)

INTRODUCTION

KEY NUMBER ONE for unlocking your power as a woman in ministry is to make clear decisions as to what you are going to do and say both about the Bible and about God when it comes to women in ministry.

Why start with the Bible in a book that hopes to give women in ministry power when the Bible is the number one reason for arguments against women in ministry? Because the Bible is indeed where it all starts. We would not be here right now, you would not be reading this book at this moment, if it were not for the witnesses to God's love for the world as recorded in scripture. A starting point matters. Furthermore, the Bible matters. As women in ministry, we can either resist its relevance, especially when it comes to affairs concerning women, women's rights, issues women face, societal norms, expectations, marital relationships, household codes, and feminism, or we can reimagine our approach. Of course, there are a number of places to land along that stated spectrum, which is why we have to spend some serious time with our own feelings when it comes to the relationship between the Bible and women in ministry—and even our personal relationship with the Bible.

The use and misuse of the Bible to justify and judge women in ministry will not go away if we ignore it. One pastor remembers, "I once had an older gentleman tell me after service [when I was a student] that I should really read 1 Timothy 2 sometime." Will you know to what he is referring? Those around you will not necessarily let it go—and so you cannot feign that it will go away. We cannot pretend that biblical arguments against women in ministry are simply out-of-date, and therefore ignorable, because these arguments based on biblical principles will only surface in other ways. While you might eschew any claims lodged in "biblical values" that question your call to ministry, the truth remains that how people engage biblical texts is an underlying issue significantly in play with most conversations around women in ministry; it is just not admitted or acknowledged. There are assumptions at work about the authority of scripture and the role of the Bible in matters of life and faith, and there are radically different views about God and operative canons within the Canon. Canon with a capital *C* is an interesting assumption itself because different denominations in Christianity propose different collections of writings. Protestant Bibles name sixty-six books as canonical whereas Catholic Bibles also include the deuterocanonical writings. Ironically, then, when people lodge such comments so as to question your ministry that begin with "The Bible says," you might respond, "To what Bible are you referring?" Failure to engage actively with the Bible when it comes to women in ministry disregards how you have come to be in ministry in the first place and may potentially cause you to overlook important biblical figures who might also accompany both you and your present-day supporters.

What follows are four areas of focus that are critical to discernment around the role of the Bible for women in ministry: the authority of scripture, the nature and function of biblical interpretation, theological imagination for God, and the importance of feminism in constructions of faith.

THE AUTHORITY OF SCRIPTURE

The problem with canonical texts is that believers tend to confuse the voice of the author with the voice of God.

—*Searching the Scriptures*

To claim your own power as a woman in ministry demands that you wrestle with the concept of the authority of scripture and how that authority functions in your life. Assumptions about the authority of scripture are operating in, and lie behind, any claims about the Bible; however, these assumptions about scripture's authority are rarely found on the surface level of the discussions. Furthermore, there is a tacit assertion that we all presume to have the same view of scripture—at the very least, the shared belief that scripture is normative. People tend to operate with the general principle that the Bible has sole authority when it comes to navigating a life of faith, yet the reality is that many other influences on faith are at work: tradition, reason, experience, and the multiplicity of contexts that exist for any believer. To assert that the Bible is the only authority for a life of faith is an untruth, in part because it assumes that the Bible is able to have meaning regardless of the contexts in which and for which it is engaged. In addition, it ignores the fact that the Bible was never a single entity in the first place but came to be representative of the ongoing conversation between God and God's people, of which we are the heirs. This conjecture has to be called out for the fiction that it is so that conversations around scripture and women in ministry can be unshackled from falsehoods. Dialogue about women in ministry that relies on so-called biblical truths will go nowhere unless these fictions are acknowledged and addressed.

There are two essential views about the authority of scripture with which most people operate, with people landing somewhere on the spectrum between these two views. The first view is an ontological view of scripture, which states that scripture has authority on its own terms because it is scripture. Period. The second view is a functional view of scripture, which holds that scripture has authority because of how it serves to provide meaning for theological imagination and discourse. The ontological view of scripture's authority is often tied to statements about the Bible's inspiration, inerrancy, and infallibility, with little to no attention given to the question of how our view of scripture might arise and should arise from scripture itself. A related claim, therefore, is that scripture is our sole authority for our understanding of God. The Bible is God's Word, dictated by God, where human agency has no other role but scribe. *Word* is deliberately capitalized to indicate something about authority or inherent holiness. The primary point of reference for this claim about scripture is 2 Timothy 3:16-17—"Every scripture is inspired by God [*theopneustos*, "God-breathed"] and is useful for teaching, for showing mistakes, for correcting, and for training character, so that the person who belongs to God can be equipped to do everything that is good." Translation challenges abound with this phrase, when the clause can be rendered as the following:

- All scripture is inspired by God
- Every scripture is inspired by God
- All scripture inspired by God is
- Every scripture inspired by God is

Moreover, this claim about scripture as inspired ignores the fact that the author of 2 Timothy is not referring to that particular epistle, but to the Hebrew scriptures. The collection of writings we now know as the New Testament was not the New Testament, let alone scripture, when the author of 2 Timothy made this assertion. Of course, this view of authority also precludes any questions on our part. Authority is assumed as unquestionable, yet, to call a text authoritative does not have to mean that we read it uncritically.

The second view of biblical authority, a functional understanding, suggests that the Bible is authoritative because it lays claim on one's life in some way. That is, the Bible is one lens through which we view, understand, or make sense of the world. To claim the authority of the Bible is to say that it helps you put into perspective or make sense of your experience of God and who you imagine God to be. In this sense, God is still active in the world, God is still speaking, and the Bible becomes a reference point for making sense of that ongoing activity and speech. The issue is not *whether* the Bible is authoritative; the more interesting and pressing question is *how* it is authoritative. In this regard, we would want to consider the fact that the Bible is authoritative because it is about God. Yet the Bible itself gives witness to God being known outside of scripture, that is, in the relationship God has with God's people. This is where the New Testament itself speaks to where we locate and how we describe the authority of scripture. The New Testament is a series of conversations about this very tension: knowledge of God has come from what is, and was, known as scripture, but now knowledge of God comes by the experience of God's presence in the incarnation.

Equally essential for thinking about the authority of the Bible is to ask whether the Bible gains its authority from "what the Bible *says* (e.g., about God and world); or in what the Bible *is* (e.g., holy, sacred, a place to encounter God); or in what the Bible *does* (e.g., sanctify, shape character, form community)."[1]

The question should be, what does the Bible actually say about itself? How does it describe what it is, what it does, what its purpose is? The answers to these questions are as individual as the writings themselves. While a basic fact, it is crucial to remember that the Bible is not a book but a library. No writing included in the Bible ever started as, imagined itself as, or aspired to be scripture. We have made them scripture by the process of canonization, and that process has made specific witnesses to God's work in the world, particular to certain times and places, normative insofar as they call for testimony of all who claim belief in God and who have their own witness of God's activity to share.

Of course, a conversation about the authority of scripture will necessarily lead to how we define God's word. The Bible is often considered to be the word (or Word) of God or God's incarnated presence in the world through Jesus Christ, but these are very different assertions. One assumes a word that comes from God; the other points to God's embodied word in the Word made flesh. The language we use in reference to the Bible is loaded with assumptions. What does it mean when we say that the Bible is the Word of God? Some claims about the Bible are often not ones that the Bible makes about itself. To make the statement that the Bible is the Word of God necessitates answering what one means by "word" and whether capitalization makes a difference in that understanding, as well as what is meant by "*of* God." The capitalization of *word* usually designates the same kind of claims about the authority of scripture that assume its inspiration, inerrancy, and infallibility.

Is it a word from God? What word? How does the Bible give witness to the function of God's word? How do you define "word"? "Word of God" is a far more complicated description of the Bible than people make it out to be, especially because we must be mindful that when we make assertions about scripture's authority, we are simultaneously making assertions about God. For example, if the Bible is one's assumed absolute authority when it comes to faith, is God then still able to be active in one's life? If the Bible is without error, does that mean that God never made a mistake or changed God's mind (Genesis 18)? Is that also true for God now? These kinds of honest discussions around the nature of God, in connection with what we think the Bible is and does, will have a far greater impact on subsequent discussions about women in ministry than if we pretend God is not involved in what we have to say about whom God calls into ministry or that ancient writings have the last say when it comes to God's vision for the church.

Any steps toward interpreting the Bible have to start with owning one's opinion on the authority of scripture. This is an essential aspect of your power as a woman in ministry. You have to be able to articulate your own view of the authority of scripture, not only so that you can share it with others, but also so that you are better able to listen to another's view. If someone holds to an ontological view of the authority of scripture, it is unlikely you will change that person's mind when it comes to interpreting the various passages used to justify arguments against women in ministry, particularly women as pastors. To know your stance on the authority of scripture will help you listen carefully to what people say about the Bible, how they describe it, and what words are used, so as to ask questions about these claims toward true dialogue and not defense. Recognizing your opinion on the authority of scripture will then help you realize when another's view is not yours and will bend the conversation toward empathy rather than estrangement.

THE NATURE AND FUNCTION OF BIBLICAL INTERPRETATION

When we get our spiritual houses in order, we'll be dead. This goes on. You arrive at enough certainty to be able to make your way, but it is making it in darkness. Don't expect faith to clear things up for you. It is trust, not certainty.

—*Flannery O'Connor*

In many respects, unlocking your power as a woman in ministry means realizing your power as an interpreter of the Bible. "Wait a minute," you say, "I'm no biblical scholar." While that may be true (at least according to those persons whose vocation is to study the Bible and generate scholarship about the Bible), you are indeed an interpreter of the Bible. People assume that you have a knowledge of the Bible that they themselves do not have. You went to seminary or divinity school. You took Bible classes. You have skills in the area of biblical interpretation. You are, by the very nature of your role, an authority when it comes to the Bible. People will look to you for a range of reasons when it comes to their own relationship with the Bible. They will want the answers toward which you can point, although it will be up to you to note that the desire for answers from the Bible is itself a statement about the Bible. They will want to know where it says what. At the same time, even though they will not be able to articulate this truth, they want help in making sense of it. Biblical interpretation should be for them as much as it is for you. To interpret the Bible is to engage in activity that tries to make meaning, which is really how we go about life in general. We are text interpreters every day, constantly trying to make sense of what we read and what we hear. We do this interpretation from our multiple contexts that are as varied as our own persons.

A significant aspect of what it means to have power in ministry is to realize the power entrusted to you with this book we call the Holy Bible. How you engage the Bible, talk about the Bible, teach the Bible, and preach the Bible will communicate to those around you not only what the Bible means to you, but also what they think it should then mean for them. None of your statements about or references to the Bible are throwaway lines. Your relationship with the Bible is critical to your effectiveness in ministry.

We relinquish a considerable amount of our power in ministry when we forget this truth, when we then allow other sources to shape the biblical imagination of those we accompany in ministry. There is certainly no dearth of opinions about the Bible, nor is there a lack of very vocal Bible interpreters who know how to get heard. If you do not talk about the Bible and what you think about it, and if you do not help those to whom you minister to read it, then they will listen to others who do. They will go elsewhere for resources to assist them in understanding the Bible, and you might not like where they end up. Where you could have been offering ways of interpreting the Bible that are generative, you instead end up having to offer correctives and band-aid solutions that never stick as well.

As a result, one of the issues for women in ministry is presenting a posture with the Bible that may run counter to what people have encountered previously. In the end, your goal is not to convince or coerce but to invite conversation. It is to help people be better readers of the Bible. It is to affirm that questions and dialogue are essential to biblical interpretation. It is to insist that agreement is not necessary to living in community. It is to encourage their own abilities and intuitions as interpreters. If your starting point with the Bible and what it says about women is to tell others just how wrong they are, you are no different from those interpreters who have told them what the Bible has to say about women in ministry. Your starting point with scripture matters significantly.

Starting Point Assumptions

It is imperative to be able to articulate for yourself and to others your starting point when it comes to scripture. This is somewhat separate from being able to determine your own opinions on the authority of scripture. It is to take the next step and say that if you understand the Bible's authority in this way, then you work with the Bible or approach the Bible in that particular way. These starting point assumptions can be summarized by one essential admission when it comes to interpreting the Bible: whether or not someone recognizes the multiple contexts of biblical interpretation. That is, those who realize that the concept of reading the Bible objectively is a myth already know that they have working assumptions when it comes to biblical interpretation. Those who reject the insistence that the Bible can only be read subjectively will assume that it is possible to interpret biblical texts void of all outside influences. In other words, your starting points when approaching the Bible are highly personal and you need to know what they are.

All biblical interpretation is contextual. It is when interpreters insist that the Bible can be read objectively—without reference to the reader's particular context—that biblical interpretation goes awry. The realization that biblical interpretation happens in multiple contexts automatically results in the recognition that multiple meanings of texts are possible. These multiple meanings also emerge because of communities of interpretation where there is profound understanding of and regard for the contexts and experiences of the other. In this regard, the "truth" of the Bible happens in conversation and community, through dialogue rather than through monologue.

At the same time, this does not mean that all biblical interpretations are acceptable. The term *acceptable* is critical here. Biblical interpretations do not end up in a vacuum but have lasting results. They have the potential to hurt and to uplift, to harm and to give hope. Interpretations are often offered without any concern with the effect or what they will end up doing. Conversation around the consequences of our interpretations of scripture is as critical as dialogue around the individual interpretation itself. Coming to terms with the seemingly limitless contexts that affect how we interpret the Bible causes many to feel dejection and defeat. If it is all relevant anyway, why bother? What's the point? How will we ever know Truth with a capital *T*?

Yet perhaps that is precisely the point when it comes to the Bible. If the Bible is God's word to us and one way that God has chosen to reveal God's self, then the point is not to arrive, but to abide. That is, when we make claims about God as word, it is important to acknowledge where and how God as word is articulated in scripture. The prologue to John's Gospel (John 1:1-18), therefore, is crucial to any assumptions made about what God as word means. The word, in the beginning *with* God, became flesh. That is, God as word is not just vocal articulation (Gen 1; the Prophets) but the presence and possibility of relationship with God. God as word is not answers or directions but an invitation to abide; "Jesus said to the Jews who believed in him, 'You are truly my disciples if you remain faithful ["to abide" in Greek] to my teaching. Then you will know the truth, and the truth will set you free'" (John 8:31-32). God as word is an invitation to relationship.

You might be saying at this point, "Who really thinks these days that we can read the Bible objectively?" The truth is that many do, especially when it comes to issues that are controversial or divisive. Rather than do the hard work of careful biblical exegesis, and exegesis of the self, the easier route is to say "the Bible says" and all other logic flies out the window.

While you will likely have many dissenters from how you view, interpret, and approach the Bible, at least you will have demonstrated the initial hard work of engaging the Bible and taking it seriously. In the end, the Bible is not that which dictates but is a conversation partner. At the same time, a conversation with someone, at least a fruitful one, requires a mutuality of knowledge. That is, you should, with respect, know your conversation partner, or at least want to learn about your partner; and you should imagine that your conversation partner knows about you or wants to know about you. When this reciprocity is lacking, then there is no conversation to be had.

In the end, helping people recognize what they bring to the process of biblical interpretation is an act of empowerment and not detriment. You are helping them to claim their own ability to interpret scripture based on their deep and abiding relationship with God. For too many years, this power has been taken away from churchgoers. The preacher or the pastor has all the answers when it comes to the Bible and he—yes, he—will tell you what they are. We are at a place now in our congregations where we need to give back this protected interpretive power to the people in the pews. They can do this, but they will need your encouragement to do so. Furthermore, it is only together that your ministry will thrive. If there is resistance or questioning on the outside of their church walls about who has the power in their congregation, are you equipping them to answer these inquiries? When someone asks your parishioners about the legitimacy of female clergy according to the Bible, will they be able to respond thoughtfully and theologically or reactively and recalcitrantly? Unlocking your own power as a woman in ministry from the perspective of the Bible maintains that you affirm the ability of all persons to view the Bible as that which might empower ministry, ordained or not.

The Bible does not like to be taken out of context any more than we do. What are these contexts? Any interpretation of scripture has to start with being a student of its historical contexts, including the political, social, and religious realities of the time in which it was written (and to which we return below). At this juncture, however, the contexts most critical to your ability to live into your power as a biblical interpreter, and to help others do the same, are individual, textual, and communal.

The Context of the Individual

Any interpretation of the Bible inevitably has to begin with the individual. Self-interpretation is absolutely crucial for biblical interpretation. Yet, this is a difficult place to start for most. It takes hard and honest work. Most of us do not want to admit how ideological we are. Truthfully, most of us do not want to admit we even have ideologies. We assume that ideologies are inherently bad, that to be ideological or to be named an ideologue presumes an uncompromising and dogmatic stance in the world. This can certainly be true. Yet, what is also true is that we all are ideologues in some way. We all have working ideologies, or philosophies and principles, if you will. The truth-telling that needs to happen in the church and in ministry is owning up to them. Biblical interpretation, especially interpretive claims that justify certain actions, systems, and practices in the church, inevitably end up going horribly askew when ideologies go unchecked or, worse, treated as though they do not exist. Somehow, and still, too many who claim the authority to interpret the Bible insist they do not bring any influences into that interpretation; that with the Bible, one is able to bracket out any biases so as to be able to read the Bible objectively.

An illustration of this truth may be helpful at this point. There is a museum in Los Angeles called the Museum of Tolerance. After purchasing your ticket for admission into the museum, you descend an escalator to get to the museum's entrance. At the entrance is a docent standing between two double doors. Over one set of double doors is the sign

PREJUDICED. Over the other set of double doors is the sign NOT PREJUDICED. The docent then invites you to choose through which double doors you would like to enter the museum. As it turns out, the NOT PREJUDICED doors are locked because we all hold prejudices. This is the first truth you learn in this museum experience. We are prejudiced, and it is a falsehood to tell ourselves that we are not. This is also true for our ideological selves, which live and function in the systems and institutions we set in place to organize ourselves, ideologies included . . . especially the church.

Practically, the first task in assessing who you are as a biblical interpreter is to begin to list all of those things that shape who you are. These include, but are not exhausted by, the following: gender, race, education, denomination, tradition, sexual orientation, demographics, health, and family. All of these factors influence who we are and therefore what we bring to any interaction with the Bible. The question becomes which of these factors are more operative than others in how you interpret your world.

Your gender shapes the way you read. Regardless of our quests for universality and equality among the Bible's readers, the truth is women will resonate with different aspects of the Bible than men. The other truth is that there have not been enough women publicly interpreting the Bible to bring these resonances into any kind of balance with what is typically and traditionally heard in (male) interpretations.

As a woman interpreting the Bible in the public context of ministry, you have an obligation to give voice to interpretations that have either not been allowed or not been uttered aloud. This does not mean that every Bible study or every sermon needs to be about women, have a story about women, or present feminine imagery for God. In fact, if this becomes the expectation about how you engage the Bible, it can quickly be assumed that interpretations that prioritize women and women's issues are the only ways in which you can talk about the Bible. At best, you are the one who talks about "women's issues." At worst, your influence devolves into an aspect of tokenism. This has to be a shared task by you and by your colleagues in ministry, regardless of gender. At the same time, if you do not tend these other voices in scripture and acknowledge publicly that there are other interpreters besides men who care what scripture has to say, there is a good chance that no one will. If you do not lift up stories about women in the Bible, preach the texts that have women characters, and look for ways to imagine God's femininity, evidence shows that little to no attention will be given to women in the Bible or feminine imagery for God. A woman in ministry has a responsibility, in part, for this tending. We would like it to be different. We would like it to be a given that we should not have to shoulder this responsibility alone. The truth is, we are not there yet, and if you do not do this work, who will?

Practically, what does this mean as an interpreter of the Bible? Some of what is presented here will be outlined further in the discussion of the role of feminism for women in ministry. At this point, for the sake of the individual context as a biblical interpreter, it means listening deeply for the voices that call from the margins. It means giving voice to those who have been silenced or who never had a voice while still recognizing what it's like to have someone who's never had your experience speak for you. It means trusting in yourself that your interpretations can make a difference. It means trusting that your voice, your voice *as a woman*, matters, and that how you fill in gaps and where you locate yourself in the biblical texts matters deeply for many, especially for the many who have only heard one voice and have never trusted their own. Our interpretations of the Bible do shape the way we live our lives, and many in our pews have not heard that their lives matter when it comes to the Bible.

The Context of the Text

The second context necessary for unlocking your influence as a biblical interpreter is the textual context of scripture. Tending the textual context as a woman in ministry begins with the basics. That is, it means first recognizing textual issues at stake in biblical interpretation, such as translational differences, canonical order, and titles given to stories. We might also consider the names of the biblical books. Ruth and Esther stand out in a very large crowd of men.

Translations are just as beholden to theological, ecclesial, and denominational commitments as the individuals who read them. Canonical inclusion and canonical order also shape how we read and interpret biblical texts. The preference for Paul, for the thirteen writings attributed to Paul in the New Testament, means that Paul's letters will tend to carry more weight in biblical arguments having to do with women in ministry than even Jesus himself. Canonical order, in which the Epistle to the Romans comes first, will suggest that it is the most important letter from Paul, even though the only reason it is first in the canon is because it is the longest (since Paul's letters are organized by length). Titles of scriptural texts give us an inflated sense of the importance of the male voice in scripture. Indeed, a renewed imagination for titles we give to stories is a powerful means by which to upend staid and stiff interpretations, especially male-centered ones. None of the titles in the Bible are original to the stories introduced, yet titles determine what we hear.

For example, consider the title "The Woman Caught in Adultery," which is typically given to the story found in John 7:53–8:1. What does this title imply? That she is "caught" suggests that it is her fault, that it is her sin of adultery that takes center stage in this tale. Yet reading forward, and for the sake of her voice and her situation, "caught" also calls attention to the fact that she is indeed caught, like an animal, and objectified. Yet, what if the story were given the title "The Hypocrisy of the Scribes and the Pharisees Exposed"? We then find ourselves reading for *their* sin, and not hers, which in fact ends up being the point of the story. Another example is the title offered for Luke 7:36-50, "A Sinful Woman Forgiven," when the dynamics of the story also include the nature of hospitality (which Simon does not offer Jesus) and who is welcome in God's kingdom.

Paying attention to the textual context of the Bible insists that you acknowledge the specificity of the writing you are using, quoting, and referring. Each scriptural text is unique in its time, place, audience, theological themes, structure, and vocabulary. For example, we have four very unique portraits of Christ in the four Gospels. The church thought it was a good idea to include four and not just one. Who Jesus is, what Jesus does, and what Jesus represents is not a uniform construct. The Gospel writers are just as biased as we are. They have particular portraits of Jesus that they seek to communicate based on their own theological commitments. It is essential to honor these diverse presentations, and the church did by canonizing all four. While setting out essential criteria for canonization in apostolicity (can the writing be connected to an apostle/disciple in some way?), orthodoxy (does the writing represent the dominant beliefs of the church about Christ?), and universality (what percentage of Christian churches were actually reading and using the writing?), the church managed also to honor a pastoral criterion—you never know what Jesus you are going to need. When, in your life of faith, do you need the Jesus of Mark, who cries out to God from the cross in abandonment? Or when do you need the Jesus of John, who willingly gives up his own life and carries his own cross, because he is God incarnate?

Tending the textual content of the Bible as a movement toward unlocking your power as a woman in ministry also means giving attention to the breadth of imagery, metaphors, descriptors, actions, and verbs that describe God. This is not just lifting up female imagery for God, but actively seeking the ways in which God's very self engages in liberation. The emancipatory acts of God are actual moments of freedom from oppression and suggest that one characteristic of God is freedom for the oppressed. We are charged with proclaiming, teaching, and living this characteristic of God not only for the sake of others but also for the sake of our own selves. Being a woman in ministry demands that God's commitment to emancipation is not co-opted by male voices. More often than not, God's desire for those in bondage to be set free is described and asserted by those who perpetuate suppression. The charge for freedom sounds empty and hollow from those who have never known domination and oppression.

Finally, taking seriously the textual context is to name the oppression and patriarchy that is inherent in the Bible because of its historical, social, religious, and political assumptions and location. The fact is, the Bible is not interested in a lot of the questions we ask it, nor is it interested in providing the answers toward which we struggle today. The rights of women, with reference to how they have been described and defined in the last two centuries, are not arenas of society for which the Bible has language.

As a result, our commitments to the themes we bring to biblical texts are admittedly more important to us than reading the Bible as explanatory.

The Communal Context

The third context worth considering along with its various facets when it comes to your own imagination as a biblical interpreter is the communal context. That is, as a woman in ministry living into her power as one who interprets the Bible, you must enter into dialogue with other interpreters. You will have to give voice to interpretations of scripture that go against centuries of previous interpretations. The entirety of the history of interpretation lies at your feet to sift through and decide which interpretations remain helpful and which interpretations are simply harmful and can no longer be heard. This is not unlike a preacher having to determine that certain biblical lections cannot be read out loud in the congregation if they will not be addressed from the pulpit. There are too many layers, too much history, and too many new contexts that make certain texts unreadable in public without clear new interpretations. Biblical hermeneutics aimed toward unlocking your power as a woman in ministry will mean challenging those interpretations that have become seemingly divine in our eyes. It will mean calling out misogynist assumptions in readings of texts and imagining new perspectives as both correctives and hoped for realities. It will mean telling the truth about how much weight we give to certain interpretations and texts and not to others. It may mean engaging in a hermeneutics of suspicion and even protest for the sake of lifting up voices that need to be heard.

Claims about the authority of scripture are lodged behind and used to justify ways of interpreting scripture. What you think about the Bible determines what you think the Bible says, does not say, and is capable of saying. That is, where you start with scripture is where you will end up. For example, if the Bible is a book of rules or a moral code for life, then the outcomes of your interpretive efforts will be a list of rules. If the Bible is a collection of concretized witnesses to the activity of God in the world, then it will be a collection of manifestations of discipleship that enable you to navigate your own life as a disciple. This truth helps the process of engaging the Bible when it comes to women in ministry because it makes the correlation between absolute claims about whether or not women should do ministry and assumptions about scripture. In other words, these claims are, more often than not, about a person's issues with scripture, rather than about their issues with you, per se.

One essential aspect for living your power as a woman in ministry is to reflect on and come to some conclusion about how the Bible and its stories have shaped your imagination as a minister. Does a particular story or character come to mind? Why that story? What is it about that character that enlivens you, gives you hope? What is it about God in this story that confirms that you are an integral part of God's ministry for the sake of the world God loves? Being able to articulate and locate yourself in these stories is imperative on several fronts. First, it locates your ministry within the larger trajectory of persons who have answered God's call. Situating your own experience within the multiple contexts and experiences of God's believers creates the necessary cloud of witnesses when your current situation seems void of those needed supporters. Second, it reveals succinctly who you think God is and in what kind of God you believe. Knowing this theological truth about yourself not only helps you to make sense of your theological leanings but also will assist you in helping others to be able to express their understandings of who God is. We make a lot of claims about who God is supposedly for or against without offering the corollary claim of what kind of God we assume God to be.

Third, being able to articulate the story or stories that have shaped you shows both you and others that approaches to interpreting the Bible do not have to result in answers. Put another way, it demonstrates to you and to others how the Bible is authoritative in your life in a different way than how the Bible's authority is typically construed, as discussed above, when it comes to women in ministry. Once again, where you begin with your engagement with scripture will determine, in part, where you end. When it comes to the Bible and women in ministry, however, we know that it is very specific biblical texts, not just general principles about biblical interpretation, that are brought to bear when it comes to women in ministry and the Bible, which is where we now turn.

Chapter One

"Those" Passages

No text that is destructive of the human and personal worth of women (or anyone else) can be the revealed word of God.

—Women's Bible Commentary

As a woman in ministry, you need to be aware of and conversant in those biblical passages that will be used against you and those that will be brought out to come to your rescue. This chapter began with discussion around the authority of the Bible because either list falls into the trap of prooftexting if you do not acknowledge the assumptions of biblical authority that lie behind them.

Any presentation of these passages, however, necessitates acknowledgment that not all people who believe in or talk about the Bible are fluent in or care about current methods of biblical interpretation. Of course, there are a number of approaches when it comes to critical methods of biblical scholarship. These methods cannot be given full representation here, but one particular principle of biblical scholarship is essential when it comes to navigating conversations around the biblical passages listed below: that of tending to the historical, social, political, and religious contexts of the biblical texts, in all their complexities. The reality is that much of how the Bible is imagined to speak to us today ignores these contexts altogether. The working assumption is that the truth of what biblical passages said to their original audiences, and how they were heard by them, is the same as how they sound to us now, with no acknowledgment of the precise contexts in which the texts were written. In this neglect is a general disregard for the particularities of issues that the original audiences of these writings were facing. The supposition, too often, is that the Bible speaks directly to us, in our time, regardless of its original location in a particular place, time, and people in history.

Another unspoken assumption is that of authorship. With Paul's dominant presence in the New Testament canon, even Jesus himself is overshadowed by Paul's apostolicity. The stories of Jesus's invitations to women to join in his ministry are altogether ignored in favor of Pauline mandates, or that of those who wrote in Paul's name. The passages that will likely surface to justify opposition for women in ministry are the following:

1 Corinthians 14:34-35. These verses calling for the silence of women in the churches have been interpreted in a number of different ways depending on the assumptions brought to the passage. Is Paul speaking about women here who are in leadership roles or women who are worshiping in the congregation? This remains the determining interpretive question that, in the end, has to be reconciled with 11:5—"Every woman who prays or prophesies with her head uncovered disgraces her head. It is the same thing as having her head shaved." If 11:5 is to be taken as women leading worship, and if 14:34-35 is also directed to women leading worship, then there is a contradiction. This has led scholars to argue that 14:34-35 are a non-Pauline interpolation added later to the letter. This has some traction when we consider the more direct misogyny of the deuteropauline corpus, that is, letters attributed to Paul, but likely not authored by Paul.

While this passage will be used as evidence against women in leadership in the church, particularly ordained positions, it is important to note the ambiguity surrounding the passage as well as the kind of argument that is being made. Just because Paul, if it is Paul, says women should be silent in the churches is not ergo a ban against their leadership. This is a common trajectory for persons attempting to argue against women's leadership in the church, that a rather vague statement about women's behavior in a worshiping congregation is automatically a statement against women's leadership in the church. A few steps have been skipped in this kind of presentation of the argument.

1 Timothy 2:8-15. While attributed to Paul, 1 Timothy is considered by scholars to represent a later canon of writings drawing on the authority of Paul but not actually penned by Paul. Unlike 1 Corinthians, which is considered one of Paul's seven undisputed letters, 1 Timothy is one of the disputed letters. This point is critical for the interpretation of these verses. One aspect of the authority of this text as conclusive for the case against women in ministry is gained by its Pauline authorship. Pseudonymity was common in the ancient world and would have been particularly important for later Christian writers to garner authority for their own writings. First Timothy represents later Christianity that begins to mold itself to the patriarchal societal structures of the Roman Empire. We might ask why it was so important for someone after Paul to use him to silence women's voices. These instructions for women suggest conformity to the androcentrism of the surrounding culture and are not representative of the larger New Testament witness to women in leadership roles in the church. Following instruction on how men should pray, these injunctions for women should suggest that women were also praying in public. The effort to silence women suggests that they were indeed praying in public and that the author seeks a change in conduct.

Essential to keep in mind for the interpretation of both of these passages are two primary suppositions at work that are rarely named in the arguments against women in ministry. First, it is assumed that these directions for women are commands for all time and all places rather than for a specific time and place, even specific congregational circumstances. They cannot automatically be considered the norm of Christian thought and practice when other New Testament passages presume women in leadership roles, which will be discussed further below (Acts 21:9; Rom 16:1-16; Phil 4:2-3). Second, while Paul dominates the New Testament, his writings are not exhaustive of the views presented on women in the New Testament. To take these passages as the quintessential cases against women in ministry is to afford them an authority that has to be explained by the interpreter. There is no reason to suggest why Paul's prescriptions should be binding and other New Testament presentations ignored, even the ministry of Jesus himself.

It is important to notice that these passages specifically call attention to positions of *public* ministry. This is a subtle, yet vital, detail because the primary locus of resistance to women in ministry roles is lodged against those women who have observed places of power or roles that put them regularly in front of people. As a result, a second tier of passages is hauled out to argue for the complete subjugation of women—to men and to society, removing them entirely from agency within the public domain. These passages include:

Ephesians 5:21-33. Critical to the interpretation of this passage from Ephesians is that it bases its description of the Christian household on the household codes of Greco-Roman society (see also Colossians 3:18–4:1) where the position of men over women would secure a functional society structure. It is widely held by scholars that the use of the household codes in Christian literature toward the end of the first century CE represents adaptation to societal expectations over the more egalitarian views of first-generation Christianity. The equality afforded women in the early stages of the church became problematic, primarily as Christianity sought to establish itself as a viable religious option. Lacking in most arguments that draw on Ephesians to justify the position of women in society and women in ministry is the reciprocity demanded by both men and women, particularly the expectations of the husband. Regardless, household structures critical for Greco-Roman culture and society are not binding for Christians, nor are they the same as how we manage our households today. To transplant this essential social unit from the ancient world to our present-day constructs of relationship is problematic, to say the least.

Genesis 1–3. The creation story becomes another biblical proof text to justify the place and roles of women in society, and therefore, in church leadership. In these interpretations, woman is seen as inferior because she was created second and is derived from man. Of course, this argument does not take into account the first creation story, only the second, and assumes certain meanings of the term *helper* that are prescribed by the interpreter and not the text itself. The primary concern of God for the man is not that he lacks a subordinate but that he needs companionship, a partner. Once the trajectory of the woman's secondary and inferior status is in place, her role in Eden is solidified as the one at fault for expulsion from the garden. The complexity of Genesis 3 and the man's role, or lack thereof, is overlooked in favor of laying the blame at the feet of the woman. The ways in which the creation story has been lodged in arguments against women in ministry reveal both sloppy exegesis and blatant sexism. Nonetheless, hiding behind claims against women in ministry are these two passages. If a woman's role in the church cannot be undermined by specific texts that seem to forbid it directly, the next best step is to wager ancient hierarchical social structures to seal the deal.

While these passages are less prevalent in arguments against women in ministry, they are still functioning so as to undergird and justify those arguments. Women simply cannot, it is argued, have that kind of power: the kind of power that might allow them to make binding decisions, that allows them to adjudicate determinations that could have an effect on the whole community, especially upon men.

Why are these particular passages prioritized while at the same time there are also biblical passages used for celebrating the roles of women in the church and individual passages where women are specifically mentioned as having leadership roles? Getting at the motivations behind choosing one set of passages over the other is crucial to knowing what is at stake for the argument at hand. Yet, determining these motivations is the harder issue because it means coming to terms with larger issues, such as the authority of scripture and theological imagination. It is never just about the Bible.

There are a number of important passages that point to women having leadership roles in the church. Knowledge of these passages, however, will do little good if they are brought out as proof texts to deflect the attack of the biblical passages discussed above. If, however, you can draw on these passages in conversation where dialogue seems possible, they can help people realize the wide variety of roles for women in the early church.

The first set of passages falls under the heading of specific women named as having ministry roles in the church. Romans 16:1-16 could easily be overlooked as simply a slew of names of people to whom Paul sends his greetings except that of the twenty-seven individuals named (twenty-nine total), one-third of them are women. Furthermore, specific leadership roles are attributed to these women: Phoebe is a deaconess (16:1); Prisca and Aquila (16:3), Mary (16:6), and Tryphaena, Tryphosa, and Persis (16:12) are all described as "workers for the Lord." Junia is the only female in the Bible named as one of the apostles (16:7). In Acts 21:9, the daughters of Philip the evangelist had the gift of prophecy. Euodia and

Syntyche in Philippians 4:2-3 have, with Paul, "struggled together with me in the ministry of the gospel."

Another set of passages would include stories of women who, while not having a designated leadership role, exemplify ideal discipleship characteristics. For example, the Samaritan woman in John 4:1-42 is a representative witness, which is a primary theme of discipleship in the Fourth Gospel. Luke 8:1-3 lists Mary Magdalene, Joanna, Susanna, and many others who accompany Jesus and the Twelve and exemplify service and hospitality. John 21:11-18 and Luke 24:1-11 name women as the first persons to announce the resurrection.

In a class by itself, however, is Galatians 3:28—"There is neither Jew nor Greek; there is neither slave nor free; nor is there male and female, for you are all one in Christ Jesus." While Paul uses Jew-Greek and slave-free in 1 Corinthians 12:13 and Colossians 3:11, the male and female (note "and," not "or") is unique to this verse. As simple as this verse appears to be, interpretations abound.[2] At the same time, however, there is perhaps no more powerful statement of gender equality, especially alongside two other hierarchical relationships that are also erased in the person and work of Christ Jesus.

What is interesting in the above summary is that blanket and seemingly generic claims about women are favored by those who discredit women in ministry while specific stories of real women in leadership positions in the church are highlighted by those who seek to support the roles of women in the church. This observation suggests a disturbing truth when it comes to this kind of argumentation: we tend toward supposedly universal truths to give authority to our human arguments, but it is in the particularity of the human response to God, and God's decision to engage in the particularity of humanity, that truth is discovered.

As a result, we see again the importance of knowing one's own working constructive theology. For example, one could use the theological claim of the incarnation to argue for the correctness of biblical witness of women in ministry. Since God entered into humanity as Jesus, since the Word became flesh, does that not, therefore, mean that God committed God's very self to the totality of what it looks like and means to be human?

At the same time, however, one could emerge from the same doctrine of the incarnation with the conviction that God entered humanity as a man, and thereby privileged the male gender as representative of God.

A perceived and preferred strategy for communication about women in ministry is to counter one proof text with another. The one with the biggest and best arsenal will win the battle. Yet, that kind of stance will hardly lead to dialogue and only to the impasse of who thinks they know the Bible better than the other. The real question is why one set of passages is more important than another in one's mind, which has everything to do with one's imagination about God. What passages win out, which texts trump others, and what conclusions we can draw from a given theological claim has less to do with extant reasoning and more to do with what's at stake for one's theology—and what one fears.

No one wins these battles. In fact, even the word *battle* is troubling. Often the suggested strategy in these kinds of circumstances is to "pick your battles." You cannot engage in every fight, so your best tool is to choose carefully those issues most important to you and that demonstrate that you have "skin in the game." The problem with these metaphors is that they are decidedly male-centered and inherently competitive. Once again, where you begin matters. If you enter into ministry from a starting place of competition, combat, and crusade, then your ministry will, by default, embody that ethos.

An alternate strategy is to know what you stand for and what's at stake for you; rather than fight for it, embody it and invite conversation around it. At the same time, that means you have to be willing to engage that conversation, at that level, with those who would rather eschew this more difficult dialogue around the authority of scripture, biblical interpretation, and theological imagination in favor of inherited answers that do not require thought or deliberation. At some point in time you may have to come to terms with the fact that conversation is not always possible, and that people will reject not only your ministry but also how you have chosen to engage, or not engage, the issue. This is typical, however, when you have determined to live out of your own truth or when you believe fully in God's commitment to your call.

The truth of the matter is that we all have a "canon within the canon." We are radically selective in what biblical writings we deem worth listening to and which we can set to the side as archaic, not for our time, not applicable, or not relevant. The only rhyme and reason for this selectivity comes back to one's own theological commitments, which is why awareness of one's working theology, or one's image of God and the characteristics that go along with that portrait, is absolutely critical. In fact, a rather large portion of believers are closet Marcionites and simply do not even know that they are. They readily and rather easily favor the New Testament over the Old Testament because their view of God gives loyalty to the "God of grace" revealed in Christian scripture as opposed to the "God of wrath" so clearly evident in Jewish scripture. Beyond the fact that such a classification of God is immanently problematic, the pitting of one Testament over another seems acceptable and reasonable. Our individual canons are just that—individual and personal, yet few people are willing to admit that this is indeed a primary operating principle for their approach to the Bible.

THEOLOGICAL IMAGINATION FOR GOD

Don't just rearrange the deck chairs on your Titanic *theology.*

—*Emilie Townes*

The truth is that any claim about God is usually a claim about scripture and any claim about scripture is usually a claim about God. Furthermore, the approach that one takes in engaging scripture has everything to do with one's understanding of God. If one contends that God calls only men and not women, only this group and not others, then what primary characteristic of God is assumed? What is your biblical imagination when it comes to how God is active in the world? The statements made about scripture reveal the central characteristics of God that are at work. At the same time, particular claims about God will lead to certain claims about the authority of scripture and the nature and function of the Bible. These are not separate categories at work, but are deeply interrelated. Our image of God informs our reading of the actual biblical text—and often trumps it. But where does this image come from?

Rather than biblical prooftexting, a more effective strategy for entering into dialogue about women in ministry is to appeal to intentional thought about God. In most conversations concerning the Bible around controversial topics, God seems like a bystander, standing off to the side observing the antics, or shaking God's head in utter consternation and bewilderment. To bring God, and our theological thinking and deliberation, into the center of these conversations raise the stakes for how one then chooses to articulate certain claims. If God is actually a conversation partner in these conversations, the tone and the direction will change.

As noted above, central to how you engage in conversation around the Bible is awareness of your theological convictions. What do you believe about God that affirms your call? What does it mean that others' views about God do not affirm your call? How will you deal with this discrepancy? What do one's statements for or against women in ministry say about their view of God? These are critical questions for you and for those to whom and with whom you do ministry.

Yet, how do you access your own theological convictions and how do you help others do the same? The first step is to acknowledge that our resources for how we think theologically are many and varied. While some will refer to the sole authority of scripture as providing their image of God, the truth is theological thinking is influenced by three primary factors: experience, tradition, and the Bible.

Experience is the sum total of one's lived realities. We experience the activity of God in the people we meet, the communities in which we choose to interact, and our own sense of how God is working in our lives. Experience is a helpful starting point in theological reflection because it taps into our fundamental belief that God is doing things in our world, God is active (regardless of how that activity is described), and God was incarnated. This is an opportunity for you to consider memories and moments where God revealed God's self in ways that, upon reflection, you now see as being God at work. The truth is, much of our theological construction is in hindsight, which is why we have to recognize that our theological convictions are cumulative.

In fact, your "call story" can be a good place to start because it will reveal how you view your relationship with God. How you understand your relationship with God will also manifest the central characteristics you value in God. One important aspect of beginning with experience in your theological reflection is that you come to realize how your theology changes over time. While we all have an acting embedded theology that functions as a foundational platform on which to base how we make sense of God in the world, this embedded theology is called into question at certain moments in our lives. These are usually crisis moments, when what you have always believed about God, how God works, and what God is up to is now unsettled, unsure.

This is crucial when it comes to negotiating the idea of women in ministry in places and with persons where this has not been an accepted practice. Part of what you are dealing with is a moment of change, when the embedded theology is now forced to move to deliberative theology.[3] This is an exceedingly difficult experience for most people because their faith—their theology—is frequently the "one thing" on which they can rely, that will not change amidst the sea of changes that life brings. When you start pulling on one card, the chance of the house collapsing is too much for most to bear. They can change, things can change, but somehow God is bracketed out, which, of course, insists on God's immutability. They need their church to stay the same when everything around them is shifting. In truth, this is a pastoral moment on your part. Even those persons who are accepting and affirming of women in ministry will likely face moments of internal theological challenge in the process. Fear surrounds the concept of the fact that one's theological thinking might change because then the correlate question is "has God changed?" Theological thinking is risky business for most and, in the end, requires a commitment to pastoral care. No one emerges better off from these kinds of conversations if the starting point was not a place of kindness.

A second major influence on how we think theologically is tradition. One way to define tradition is through the lens of denominationalism.

Each denomination has it its own dominant view of God that is operative in its polity, confessions, worship, and rituals. Each denomination has a canon within a canon because these writings best describe how God is imagined in its church structures and commitments. Your denominational history has a major impact on how you think theologically. Your denominational practices have shaped your view of God, and a denominationally framed God often trumps a biblically based God. This is not a negative reality; it is just real and has to be admitted. Doctrinal and confessional statements about God deeply influence one's theological imagination and also determine one's approach to and reading of scripture.

It is critical to be able to name the traits assigned to God that seem to be denominationally driven and why they have such power. Moreover, denominational imagination about God gets fixed, and it is often a point of challenge as a woman in ministry. What gender is God, according to our denominational theology/polity? When and how is female imagery of God raised up? Imagination for what a pastor looks like and sounds like is very much still in play and determined by denominations that reject women in leadership roles. What's at stake theologically in these claims? How are they connected to the sacramental system of the denomination, if any? This also becomes a critical act in contextual analysis. How does a denomination or a particular congregation talk about God? What are the dominant images or metaphors in use? How do they define major theological concepts such as sin, salvation, and atonement? When you engage in individual conversations with people, these are the kinds of things for which to listen. A helpful taxonomy by which to access your theological commitments, and those of others, is as follows:

1. Answer theological questions: What is God up to? Who is God? Of course, another way to get at what God is up to is from our own perspective. That is, what do we need that God provides? What is the human condition, brokenness, and sin that we need God to address? How you imagine your own needs, your own sin, and your own condition and brokenness will, in part, determine who you need your God

to be. For example, if you are plagued by a need for forgiveness, then God's primary role is as Forgiver, the one who forgives sins.

2. Answer christological questions: What has Christ done for us? What does Christ continue to do for us? What is essential to your portrait of Christ?

3. Answer soteriological questions: What is salvation or atonement? What does salvation look like? When is salvation?

4. Answer eschatological questions: What does a future life with God look like?

5. Answer ecclesiological questions: What is church? Who defines church? What does the body of Christ look like?

6. Ask pneumatological questions: Who is the Holy Spirit? What defines the primary activity of the Holy Spirit?

The more time you spend thinking about and reflecting on your own theological convictions, the better positioned you will be to lay out your own arguments for women in ministry. You will have to have an argument for yourself and be able to articulate these arguments clearly and concisely because others will have their own arguments, both in support of and in resistance to women in ministry. At the same time, this is not about being argumentative. This is not about justification. This is about being able to express clearly your own sense of how God has called you and why. Otherwise you will adopt another's position and assume he or she is right.

Another feature of tradition, in addition to denominationalism, is the default to tradition for the sake of tradition. There are a number of issues that surface in this category of which women in ministry, and the people with whom they work and serve, need to be aware. The first has to do with perceptions of clergy. An old argument holds that if Jesus was a man, then clergy have to be male. There is little logic connected to this claim, yet that does not seem to matter in these conversations. A similar statement will be made that since the twelve disciples were all male, then clergy should be men, regardless of the fact that there are references to female followers (Luke 8:1-3) and that female characters in the New Testament are portrayed as models of true discipleship (Luke 1; John 4:1-42; 20:11-18).

But again, this has everything to do with one's starting point and assumptions. Consider the following quote:

> The Archbishop [Joseph L. Berardin] insists that the natural resemblance between Christ and his priests must not stop merely with the fact that they share a common masculinity. Our question is, "Why must it BEGIN there?" If the faithful cannot see Christ in a male who exemplifies no godlike virtues—humility, gentleness, and self-effacing service—can they not see him in a female who does? Indeed, if the priest acts "in persona Christi," not "in masculinitate Christi," then "NATURAL resemblance" between Christ and the priest, it would seem, does not entail PHYSICAL, that is SEXUAL resemblance, but a resemblance which is natural to the SPIRITUAL order with which the worshiping congregation has to do. And in this order there is neither male nor female, even as there is neither Jew nor Greek. We would, therefore, conclude that since the Word was made flesh, as the apostle John has declared him (John 1:14), we rightly heed those who, in the flesh, symbolize his presence as they speak and act in his name. But we see no reason to add to what the apostle said by insisting that the Word was made MALE flesh, for both male and female are equally bearers of the divine image. And since God created humankind in his image, male AND female, we can only conclude that women as well as men should be ordained to the priesthood, because femaleness, like maleness, is a fitting symbol (sacramental sign) of Deity.[4]

There is also the important realization that even though some denominations have been ordaining women for years, even decades, there is still almost two thousand years of tradition that stands behind male representation for God. How tradition gets used, and what it is assumed to be, needs to be on your radar as a woman in ministry. You will need to be observant of arguments that tie women in ministry, in a negative fashion, to other kinds of leadership, usually "less desirable" (read: traditional), in the church. For example, cases are made in comments about the ordination of gay and lesbian persons that "the first domino" in this trend toward "unconventional" leadership in the church was the ordination of women. The implication is that women's ordination was the downfall of the church, the act that let loose the floodgates to anyone being ordained, the Pandora's box that opened up the innocent and otherwise holy church to anyone wanting to be a pastor. As women in ministry, this calls forth a responsibility toward a stance of solidarity and community with those persons the church continues to deem suspicious as possible ministers in the church. We stand on the shoulders of those women who came before us. How will we be those persons on whom others might rely to help navigate the terrain of "unconventional" ministry? Do we present ourselves as ones grateful for the opportunity to come alongside those whose call is denied, even rejected, or do we insist on some kind of entitlement for that which we have suffered?

A third factor in how we think theologically is, of course, the Bible. One way to access the diversity of theological thinking in the Bible itself is to ask the theological questions, listed above, of a particular biblical text. Take any story in the Bible and ask these questions: What is God up to in this text? Who does God seem to favor and why? Who do I want God to favor? Who is Jesus in this story, and what has he done for me? What is the picture of salvation being portrayed in this text? From what or for what am I being saved? What do "heaven and hell" look like in this text? How is the community of believers being described in this story? What is the Holy Spirit up to in this text?

At the same time, one of the most important questions to ask of a given biblical text—that has everything to do with women in ministry—is, what is the called-for response to the gospel that is outlined or implied in this story? What does the text say about living out our faith? What does this text have to say about living life in the presence of God? Is there a called-for response to what God has done? How does the text speak about being a disciple of Jesus? What does discipleship look like? What is being asked of me, my community, and my church?

By asking these kinds of theological questions of the Bible, we begin to realize the extraordinary diversity of the scriptures. This is an important strategy when it comes to talking about the Bible and women in ministry because the frequent line to question or reject the idea of women in ministry is "Well, the Bible says . . ." Of course, what needs to follow that statement are the questions "Where? When? Why? To whom?"

Summary

The sheer number of biblical and theological arguments for and against women in ministry can be overwhelming. You will need to know the basics, which is the primary rationale for this first chapter and the first key to unlocking the power of being women in ministry. You cannot go into ministry believing or hoping that any of these issues have disappeared or that the church is now "past" such things. It isn't, and an essential strategy for handling this inevitable disappointment is not to be surprised when these justifications, both for you and against you, come your way. In the end, you need to know what's at stake *for you* biblically and theologically. If you cannot articulate an understanding of your biblical imagination, or a case that presents your theological rationale when it comes to women in ministry, you will find yourself in situations where you are left speechless about your own sense of call. You will read and hear every possible biblical argument, every imaginable theological reasoning, both in praise of you and opposing you, but in the end you have to come up with your own. No one will do this for you. And if you leave it to others to justify your call, at best, you might not resonate with their answer, even resent it because it is not yours, and at worst, take it to heart and leave the ministry altogether, despite God's call.

In very practical terms, this means you have to devote some serious time to discovering, expressing, and even rehearsing where your own story intersects with God's story. Ideally, it will start with a story from the Bible because this is where it all began. At the same time, that biblical passage may not be one that shares a story of acceptance but of rejection to which you had to say no. Furthermore, it may be that who you imagine God to be is not represented in the collection of books we call scripture. If that is the case, you need to know that about yourself and be able to tell others why this is the case and why you operate with a faith whose scriptures do not show you a God you recognize. You have to be able to voice what's at stake for you, perhaps not only to justify your call, but to invite others to voice their own.

It also means that you need to listen carefully to how others who have gone before you have done the same. One of the most important aspects of entering into ministry is to listen to the stories of others. It is very likely you already know who these people are, these people who have not only helped you to live into this call to ministry, but also have made you the theologian you are now. We gather bits and pieces of these people along the way. Listening to and reflecting on these persons in your life when it comes to how they communicate their own biblical and theological imagination for being a woman in ministry will make an extraordinary difference.

A FEW WORDS ABOUT FEMINIST BIBLICAL AND ECCLESIAL CRITICISM

Feminism isn't about making women stronger. Women are already strong. It's about changing the way the world perceives that strength.

—*G. D. Anderson*

Your understanding of and views on feminism need to be in conversation with your biblical imagination and your theological convictions. The possibility of women in ministry stands not only on the backs of those women who sat in seminary classrooms as the only female student, those women who joined church staffs as the only female staff person, and those women who had to ask that their calls be validated, but also on the promises of the feminist movement. Developments in the church parallel developments in our society and in our cultural contexts. The church's views about the Bible, God, and the persons who are in its places of power do not come to fruition in a vacuum. They are deeply affected by trends, but more so, by how our societies change in their thinking.

The importance of the feminist movement cannot be overstated when it comes to women in ministry. While an exhaustive presentation of the history of feminism is beyond the scope of this book, a review of the principles of feminist biblical criticism, along with feminist critique, is essential for the evaluation of interpretations of biblical texts and systemic ecclesial practices that continue to marginalize women. Feminist biblical scholarship has given voice to those persons and principles that call for the emancipation of all people. Were we to rely solely on the passages where women actually get to speak so as to imagine our place in God's church, we would quickly deplete our sources. The actual words spoken by women in the Bible is somewhere around 14,000 and "the words of Bible women could be uttered in less than two hours" by the standard pace of speech.[5]

A woman entering ministry is indebted to women biblical scholars who took up the Bible and offered a different perspective. At its core, feminist biblical criticism, like the feminist movement, called out the injustices of persons in the texts overlooked, marginalized, taken for granted, and silenced, as well as the interpretations that perpetuated these injustices. Of course, the range of approaches in feminist biblical criticism is broad, and it is important to respect this diversity. For some feminist critics, the Bible still can have a voice in the life of faith and in the workings of the church despite its inherent patriarchy. For others, the Bible can no longer be a resource for theological imagination because of both its inherent patriarchy and the ways in which it continues to be used to justify the oppression, subjugation, and harmful treatment of women and others. As a woman in ministry, this knowledge is essential, particularly as you adjudicate biblical commentary or conversations on the authority of scripture.

Furthermore, to what extent will you, as a woman in ministry, seek to tend this history and carry it forward? That is to say, if the overwhelming majority of interpretations of biblical stories have been created out of a white, Anglo-Saxon, male-dominant narrative, a major corrective is necessary to represent the breadth of people who read and hope to hear God's word in scripture, including women. Forty years cannot erase centuries. We are just getting started. What does this actually look like when it comes to biblical interpretation? It looks like recognizing how we fill in gaps and let silenced voices be heard. Where we locate ourselves in the biblical text matters for how a biblical story is experienced—a hermeneutic of pluralism, if you will. It looks like preaching, teaching, and speaking regularly about the simultaneous unity and diversity that is present in the Bible. It means coming from a place of questions for the Bible, rather than always assuming it has answers; it means that we acknowledge its complexities on a consistent basis. Awareness of the intersections of the Bible and feminism also necessitates talking about the fact that interpretations of passages are not without significant levels of subjectivity and they will then exist beyond our controlled efforts. They affect us and others, and they shape the way we live our lives. We have to be willing to dialogue and admit that we give some interpretations more weight than others, and why we do that in the first place.

Feminist biblical criticism is essential as a woman in ministry because it has exposed the truth that any hermeneutic will be seen as objective, even divine, if it is not challenged; that hermeneutics is not the same as divine revelation, and that the two have to be separated permanently. Feminist biblical criticism brings to the interpretive table the permission to imagine hermeneutics not as an exercise in answers but as an act of protest, of suspicion, and that this suspicion can legitimately lead to either the rejection of a text or its redemption.

It is important that the beginnings of feminism were quickly determined not to be representative of all women. In fact, feminism was a white, privileged movement that needed its own correctives in Womanist, Mujerista, Asian, and lesbian feminist movements. Necessary in the evaluation of feminist biblical criticism is to insist that it is no more and no less ideological than any approach to scripture. Any and all biblical criticism is ideological, but the dominance of one, for these many years, makes it harder to see. A white, male, Anglo-Saxon interpretation that has dominated the field of biblical criticism is just as ideological as any marginalized interpretation. But the larger, dominant, assumed contexts are always the hardest to see and acknowledge.

One helpful strategy for engaging feminist principles in your ministry is to look for ways to provide a feminist theological imagination in your preaching and teaching. In doing so, you are inviting conversation around feminism, faith, and theology in a nonthreatening way, one that comes from the sidelines rather than as a direct address. This might include preaching on feminist imagery of God, making sure you teach and preach those passages that describe God in more female categories. At the same time, tending to feminism in your ministry is also an oblique exercise. It means giving voice to those who have none and freeing those who have been in captivity far too long because of their gender.

CLOSING THOUGHTS

The first key to unlock your power as a woman in ministry has to be about the Bible. It is the Bible, both its content and how it has been interpreted, that remains as the primary stumbling block to the church's imagination for who can serve as its ministers. Your relationship with the Bible and knowledge of the issues at stake articulated in this chapter will not only be an essential factor when it comes to questions about your call but also so as to affirm your sense of call. Your silence about the Bible when it comes to your leadership role in the church will only serve as proof that the Bible is not relevant for our lives today, will suggest that you have not done the hard work of engaging scripture, and will even undermine the understanding of the authority of scripture that you are hoping to challenge and embody.

EXERCISES AND QUESTIONS FOR REFLECTION

1. Think of a story from the Bible that you can connect to your own sense of what it means to be a woman in ministry. Why this story? Who are you in the story? What does this story reveal about God with which you resonate?

    Consider this example from a pastor: "I recall the words of Jeremiah 1:5-8, 'Before I formed you in the womb I knew you before you were born I set you apart; I appointed you as a prophet to the nations...You must go to everyone I send you to and say whatever I command you…Do not be afraid of them, for I am with you and will rescue you,' declares the LORD.' They were the words I read in my Bible on a hot night in Ecuador seven years ago when I felt called to become a preacher. Words that I specifically chose to be read at my ordination. Words that I must remind myself of over and over again when the lie 'God would never choose you' grows to be too loud inside my head."

2. Recall a time when you have witnessed the Bible/theology being used to justify/support certain claims about women in the church. What passages were quoted? Where did the conversation end up? What feelings surfaced in the interaction? How did you handle it?

3. Consider the operative influences on your theological imagination—tradition, experience, and scripture. Which holds the most weight and why?

RESOURCES FOR BIBLICAL INTERPRETATION, THEOLOGICAL REFLECTION, AND FEMINIST STUDIES

If you have only one book on your shelf as a reference for feminist biblical interpretation, it needs to be Carol A. Newsom, Sharon H. Ringe, and Jacqueline E. Lapsley, eds., *The Women's Bible Commentary*, 3rd ed. (Louisville: Westminster John Knox, 2012).

See also:

Sarah Bessey, *Jesus Feminist* (New York: Howard Books, 2013).

Rita Nakashima Brock and Rebecca Ann Parker, *Proverbs of Ashes* (Boston: Beacon, 2001).

Jennifer D. Crumpton, *Femmevangelical: The Modern Girl's Guide to the Good News* (St. Louis: Chalice, 2015).

Elisabeth Schussler Fiorenza, ed., *But She Said: Feminist Practices of Biblical Interpretation* (Boston: Beacon, 1992).

————, ed. *Searching the Scriptures: A Feminist Commentary* (New York: Crossroad, 1994).

Linda Day and Carolyn Pressler, eds., *Engaging the Bible in a Gendered World* (Louisville: Westminster John Knox, 2006).

Letty M. Russell and J. Shannon Clarkson, eds., *Dictionary of Feminist Theologies* (Louisville: Westminster John Knox, 1996).

Luise Schottroff, Silvia Schroer, and Marie-Theres Wacker, eds., *Feminist Interpretation: The Bible in Women's Perspective* (Minneapolis: Fortress, 1998).

Marion Ann Taylor, ed., *Handbook of Women Biblical Interpreters* (Grand Rapids: Baker, 2012).

KEY NUMBER TWO

THE TRUTH ABOUT VULNERABILITY, BODIES, AND SEXUALITY

this is my body given for you

This is my body
This is my broken, scarred, squishy body
      —a slave to this sinful and fallen world
"Wretched woman that I am! Who will release me from this body of death?" [Rm. 7]
This is my body that I have hated—judging every inch, roll, wrinkle and stretch mark
It's never been a perfect body, but it's mine.
This is the body of muscle and strength that I have loved—using it to skate and run and
    dance in my Jammies to Mariah Carey and Frozen
There is really nothing special about it, but it's mine.
This is the body that grew new life in its womb. It stretched and bulged and deflated in ways
    so that it will never be the same again,
This same body flowed with milk and honey [well, mostly milk], creating a promised land to
    sustain new life.
There is nothing original about it, but it is mine.
This is my body. By itself it is extraordinarily unimpressive. Filled with falleness and sin, and
    the scars to prove it.
This is my body, but it's not just mine, because there is a New Creature within it—something
    completely apart from myself, deep within the fleshy sinew, my sarx
—is a Promise.
Inside this body is a voice that cried out from heaven, Rebecca Lynn, I have created you. I
    have called you by name, you are mine. You are precious and honored in my sight and I
    love you. [Isaiah 43] This Promise formed me in my inward parts; it knit me together in
    my mother's womb. This body was fearfully and wonderfully made. [Psalm 139]
On its own, it is nothing. Subject to death, and doomed to return to the dust from which it
    came.
But with the Promise, and because of the Promise, I am more than just my body.
I am a vessel. Called and sent to go out, to preach the Word of God. I am not ashamed, but
    have sufficient courage so that now as always Christ will be exalted in my body, whether
    by life or by death. (Philippians 1)
Because of the Promise, the gift of Grace, and the redemption of the cross, I am more than
    this body
and this body is not mine.
It is the Lord's.
How beautiful that this vessel can be all at once the worst of the sinners and the greatest
    of the saints. How wonderful that, through the death of Jesus Christ on the cross, who
    sacrificed *his* body, I may be saved.
And wanna know something great? Christ has saved you too. You are the vessel of the Lord,
    too. Your body, no matter what the shape, size, ability or squishiness is redeemed and
    you have been made anew! Hallelujah! Death where is thy victory, where is thy sting? [1
    Corinthians 15]
If Christ is in you, though the body is dead because of sin, yet the spirit is alive because of
    righteousness. But if the Spirit of Him who raised Jesus from the dead dwells in you, He
    who raised Christ Jesus from the dead will also give life to your mortal bodies through his
    Spirit who dwells in you. [Romans 8]
The Word became flesh and dwelt among us. And so, my sisters and brothers in Christ, the
    Word also becomes flesh in you. And the Word became flesh for you. My flesh and my
    heart may fail, But God is the strength of my heart and my portion forever. [Psalm 73]
This is my body, given for you.
Amen.
—Rebecca Holland (Women in Ministry student)

INTRODUCTION

KEY NUMBER TWO for unlocking your power as a woman in ministry is to embrace vulnerability and, in doing so, risk the exposure of true embodiment and the expression of your own sexuality.

KEY NUMBER TWO follows KEY NUMBER ONE with significant deliberation. Key number one sought to ground an understanding of your power as a woman in ministry in your relationship with the Bible and how you think theologically. One of the goals of the first key was for you to see that your call to ministry cannot be legitimized solely by outside affirmation, whether that ends up being individual people, congregations, the church as a whole, or the world. It is necessary to be able to speak about your call with a biblical and theological rationale, not for the sake of argument or justification against those who would use the same against your call, but for your own sense of how the Bible functions in your life. Too much of how we talk about issues such as women in ministry exposes a disturbing bifurcation of the Bible and God. We draw on and refer to the Bible for the claims we attempt to make while at the same time overlooking what our biblical rationales say about who we think God is. An important task of ministry, especially as a woman in ministry, is to act toward a reunification of the Bible's teachings and our assertions about God.

Furthermore, the nature of power as a woman in ministry has to be categorically different than the kind of power as a woman in secular leadership. Crucial to unlocking your power as a woman in ministry is demonstrating that you understand that difference and recognize that power in the church can and should be different from power in the world. In order to demonstrate this understanding, the entire premise of this book has to be based on biblical and theological imagination, as does your way of revealing yourself and your power. Otherwise, your power is no differ-ent from that which the world esteems.

If the first key to unlocking your power as a woman in ministry is to claim your identity as one with authority to interpret the Bible and to talk about God, then the second key to unlocking your power as a woman in ministry is to decide *how* you will talk about God. While you can choose to talk about God in many ways, all of which might find their validation in scripture, you need to choose carefully. And to be a woman in ministry means that you will need to talk about characteristics of God that will be less than popular to most, perhaps not a God they are will-ing to embrace. You will need to talk about the power of God, not only as it manifests in "typical" ways that are recognizable by the world: acts of domination, battle, and violence. But you will also need to talk about how God's power is also experienced and revealed in weakness, in lowli-ness—and in vulnerability.

You will have to question given constructions of strength and offer alternatives to what it means to be strong. You will have to present a God that is less talked about, less accepted, and even resisted. Why? Because this is the God we know. This is the God that stands in the vulnerable places and positions into which women continue to be socialized. It is not that we are inherently more vulnerable, but it is the reality to which we have had to become accustomed. This is where the world wants women to be and assumes women like to be. The truth is, the world itself is a vulnerable place, but we pretend that it isn't, especially when it comes to faith and religion. Our language about faith tends toward expressions of strength and protection rather than acknowledgment of weakness and exposure. When weakness is touted as positive, it is also used to justify and glorify positions of weakness. The working assumption is that those in perceived positions of weakness both want to be there and are content to be there. While God praises such folks, God's very self, however, es-chews a position of lowliness. God might have regard for the lowly, the overlooked, the weak, the vulnerable, but God does it from a place of privilege, not from a place of solidarity and knowledge.

Of course, vulnerability is not equivalent to weakness as we continue to want to imagine and assume. Vulnerability is recognizing that we are all not as strong as we want people to think. And women know much about vulnerability because there are many who do not want us to be as strong as we are. We might also say that our vulnerability has been exploited. This means that we are uniquely situated to speak into and about the vulnerability of faith and the vulnerability of God. You have to be willing to talk about vulnerability and the vulnerability of God, and embrace vulnerability in your ministry. As a result, the first part of this chapter begins with a biblical imagination for vulnerability and ends with discussion on the importance of recognizing the deep-seated fear that the church has around vulnerability. There are many ways in which vulnerability plays out in ministry, but a woman in ministry must absolutely have a sense of the connection between vulnerability, bodies, and sexuality. The second part of this chapter will discuss our bodies and our sexuality in light of the presentation of and assumptions about vulnerability.

A BIBLICAL AND THEOLOGICAL RATIONALE FOR THE NECESSITY OF VULNERABILITY IN MINISTRY

The Bible is not simply a history of God, but a revelation of God. God repeatedly reveals who God is—at different times, places, and purposes in the lives of God's people. God is constantly putting God's self out there—exposing, revealing, for all to see, to be the object of rejection and hurt. In fact, God seems quite intent on discovering new ways of revealing God's self, which is certainly one facet by which the New Testament writers presented the life, ministry, death, and resurrection of Christ. To reveal one's self is an act of vulnerability, which, as a result, becomes inherent to the nature of God.

To claim vulnerability as an essential characteristic of God, one could choose from a number of places in scripture that give testimony to God's own commitment to vulnerability: the call of Abraham and Sarah, the giving of the covenant, the wilderness wanderings, the prophets, Jesus, or the mission to the Gentiles. All of these examples point to the fact that our God is a God of relationship. Relationships are, by definition, vulnerable things, requiring mutuality and interdependence. Throughout the scriptures, God continues to figure out how to start relationships, keep relationships, and restore relationships—all of which require a continually renewed dedication to vulnerability.

If we are honest, the humanity of God truly informs our imagination about God far less than the divinity of God, with the exception of the crucifixion. The humanity of God is operable and acceptable when we imagine the Passion of Jesus, but how it shapes our theological conversations in between is questionable. The emphasis on the crucifixion of Jesus, not only as the primary location of atonement but also as that which affirms Jesus's humanity, is difficult when it comes to being a woman in ministry. Even Paul's soteriology can be challenging for many in ministry, not just women. Power that is perfect in weakness is problematic when it is your gender that has always been called the "weaker sex."

Unlocking the power of being a woman in ministry means that you need to give attention to how you understand and talk about salvation, particularly the cross. In other words, it is essential that you come to terms with how the cross of Christ plays a role in your understanding of God's salvific activity (or if it does not). Why? Because for too long women in ministry have had to accept or acquiesce to doctrinal claims about salvation that are located in convictions about power and suffering: suffering is to be expected, abuse is defended, weakness becomes that which justifies the stance that a woman's inferiority is perceived as positive in the eyes of God. Furthermore, it is imperative as a woman in ministry that you learn to talk about the cross as more than the moment of atonement, but also as a critique of the abuses of power, empire, and those in power who would silence those who could potentially challenge their power. In fact, it can be true that salvation is located and known in the very act of critique itself.

That is, unlocking your power as a woman in ministry means that you have to come to understand the cross on your own terms and not those set by ecclesial, doctrinal, denominational, or institutional commitments. This does not mean that you abjure the cross as central, but that you acknowledge that it is not the only means by which scripture gives witness to God's salvific activity. Moreover, for our sisters in faith who are not Christians, the privileging of the cross makes relationship and discourse more challenging. There are other images of and witnesses to the vulnerability of God besides the cross, and we are called to convey the breadth of that testimony, not only for the sake of our own authenticity, but also for the sake of those who need to hear a different story.

In fact, if we take the incarnation seriously, the death of Jesus is just that—death. Death itself is an extraordinarily vulnerable event. Yet death is the inevitable end to the incarnation. Theologically, this means that attention to the fullness of the incarnation itself is also critical for what vulnerability in ministry looks like. This suggests that we take seriously what biblical claims are made about the incarnation and that we are able to talk about the significance of the incarnation in between Christmas and Easter.

THE VULNERABILITY OF THE INCARNATION

The best place to start unpacking the vulnerability of God is the incarnation: God became human. That statement should be nothing short of earth shattering when it comes to understanding yourself as a woman in ministry. When you imagine the doctrine of the incarnation not as a doctrine, per se, but as God's commitment to the inherent vulnerability of humanity, the focus of God's intention for humanity shifts exponentially. That is, an essential component of how we understand ministry in God's church is intimately tied to God's commitment to the entirety of what it means to be human. We have a tendency to relegate major characteristics and commitments of God to doctrinal claims that keep God at bay. But that ought to be far more difficult when it comes to the incarnation.

That God chose to become human should be cause for serious pause. The birth stories carry with them their own intimations of the meaning of vulnerability. We give due attention to thinking about God as a baby around Christmastime, but that embodiment of God is frequently left behind, packed away with the Advent candles. We just get started with considering God as one who is birthed and gives birth, who risks shame and rejection for the sake of the incarnation, who chose to be located within the body of a woman, only to move on, out of liturgical necessity, but perhaps more so out of a desperate need to ease the discomfort with vulnerability connected to being a woman. It needs to be acknowledged that the majority of our imagination around God's vulnerability then fast-forwards to the cross. As women in ministry, part of our calling needs to be our willingness to speak about and even embody God's vulnerability as expressed in and known by women's bodies—and by a woman's body.

There is no other biblical writing that captures the significance of the incarnation for our theological imagination more than the Gospel of John; careful exegetical consideration of the prologue to John's Gospel (John 1:1-18) suggests that any conversation around vulnerability when it comes to ministry has to take into account God's own.[1] There are two essential exegetical and theological points that need attention when it comes to understanding vulnerability and ministry according to the first chapter in John. The first is John 1:14—"The Word became flesh and made his home among us," the Word (capitalized here to refer to Jesus). The potential understandings of "Word" in the context of John range from God's wisdom to the Greek *logos*. But there is no reason to think that the power of God's word from creation does not lie behind this claim. God's word, God's speech, brings the world into existence. God's word creates. A primary characteristic of God is to create the possibility of new creation. If that is an inherent characteristic of God, then we should anticipate this about God going forward. God is constantly creating anew.

God's word calls into being new things. Given this truth about God, God is about constant new creation. God is about the ways in which God imagines new means of God's revelation and proclamation of God's love. God's Word became flesh. Flesh. Not man, not body (*soma*) but flesh (*sarx*). Not Jesus, but flesh. All flesh. As such, the entirety of what it means to be human is at stake. God entered into the wholeness of humanity and not just a particular gender. In doing so, God honors and gives glory to the full expression of humanity. This means the experience of gender, but it also means the full spectrum of the experience of what it means to be human.

The second part of this verse is that God's Word "made his home" "lived," "dwelt," or "tented" among us. As God committed to accompany God's people wherever they were, even in the wilderness, God then chose to be among God's people as Jesus. But more, as God promised to be wherever God's people are, in becoming flesh God chose to be *who* we are—all of who we are. A woman in ministry needs to remember this truth: that if we take the incarnation seriously, God has committed God's self to the whole of what it means to be human. There is no partial humanity or selectively being human. Once we say that God is represented only in men, we have to question then what the incarnation actually means. As noted in the discussion on KEY NUMBER ONE, when we make assertions about God's activity, we are also making assertions about the fundamental nature of God. If we say that the ministry of God, that God's love toward the world, can only be carried out by men, then that calls into question the fundamental claim of the incarnation.

God knew what God was getting into. God has a very long history in dealing with humanity. It is unlikely that God was not completely aware of the full spectrum of what it means to be human, yet God decided that the incarnation was a good idea. If we doctrinalize the incarnation as gendered, we discount the history God has had with God's people. Jesus's ministry will be about demonstrating the full experience of what God's grace is when it dwells among us. For John, God, in becoming flesh in Jesus, has committed God's self not only to revealing what God's grace looks like (John 1:16), but that God wants to know it and feel it as well. While the source of our experiences of grace is most certainly God, we do not take the incarnation seriously if we think God is unaffected by those experiences. The fact that God decided to become human cannot, by definition, be a one-sided pledge. To be human means engaging in mutuality, reciprocity, and empathy. This has extraordinary implications for how we do ministry. To assert this fundamental reality about the human reality and condition is an important counter to interpretations of Jesus that are preoccupied with the divine Jesus (omnipotent, surreal, and seemingly untouchable) but also to views of God that sideline God from the very real challenges of human existence.

John 1:18 is central to a biblical imagination for vulnerability and for women in ministry. This concluding verse of the prologue to John's Gospel is a recapitulation of the claims made in John 1:1—"In the beginning was the Word" (the origin of Jesus; Jesus comes from God); "the Word was with God" (Jesus's origins were in relationship with God); and "the Word was God" (Jesus's very identity is God, revealed). In John 1:18, "God the only Son" (Jesus's identity), "who is at the Father's side" (what Jesus's relationship with God is all about) who "has made God known" (origin, because who Jesus is, is a revelation of God).

The first clause, "It is God the only Son," is the first statement of the sentence and restates the identity of Jesus made clear in the last clause of 1:1. The declaration of Jesus's identity is complicated by a translation issue and by a text critical issue. The translation issue centers on *monogenēs*, rendered in different versions as "the unique," "the one and only," and "the begotten." The identity of Jesus is once again God, as stated in 1:1, "and the Word was God," but further clarified that the Word made flesh is a unique God, a one and only revealing or representation of God, calling attention to the limits of the incarnation, but also to the uniqueness of who Jesus is. The text critical issue is the word "Son" included in some translations. The earliest and most reliable Greek manuscripts of the Gospel of John do not include the term "Son." Scribes most likely added it later, in hopes of taming or making more sense of John's radical claim. While it is true that Jesus is God's Son, and that the Father/Son relationship will become front and center after the prologue when the Word has become flesh, that is not the focus here. Jesus is God revealing God's self in a new and profoundly different way. Translations have sought to domesticate this central theological claim, yet the prologue will not let us go without another prompt that the answer to the question of Jesus's identity is always, for this Gospel, the promise that Jesus is God and fully divine.

The next two clauses in this final sentence of the prologue reiterate Jesus's origin. "From where does Jesus come?" surfaces as a critical question throughout the narrative, in part because it provides another way to answer Jesus's identity. The location of Jesus as the unique and one and only God as "close to the Father's heart" (NRSV) communicates that relationship, origin, and identity are, in fact, intimately connected and reciprocal. Why is this central to a biblical imagination for women in ministry? Because even the Word made flesh is tied to the very origins of God, who defies gender. Jesus's identity is the very presence of God, not a version of God as a male human. Furthermore, John 1:18 presents a relationship with Jesus and God that is profoundly feminine. While the majority of translations will describe the relationship between Jesus and God as Jesus being at the "side" or "heart" of God, the most accurate translation of the term is "bosom," used only one other time, in John 13:23 (NKJV), to introduce the beloved disciple.

A comparison of translations exposes a troublesome interpretive issue. The choice of "side" and "heart" over "bosom" suggests an essential difficulty with the concept that Jesus, as God's unique expression of God, and God's son, is at the bosom of the father. Margaret Miles, in her study of the breast as a religious symbol in art,[2] argues that before 1750 a primary image for salvation was the infant Jesus nursing at the exposed breast of Mary. The believer, in viewing this image, would be invited to imagine being in Jesus's position, and in doing so, experience the salvific act of God as nurture. The year 1750, however, marks two critical events in the history of humanity that have since altered our perception of this image as a possible depiction of God's love for God's people: the advent of medical anatomy and of pornography. When the female body moves from being a source of nourishment and life to becoming a detached object of study and desire, there is no longer the possibility of imagining God as embodying the feminine, and the breast as a religious symbol becomes impossible. As a result, the primary representation of salvation in art after the discoveries of anatomy and pornography becomes the crucifixion.[3]

Translations of John 1:18 after 1750 represent this remarkable shift in perception of the body, particularly the female body. To depict Jesus nursing at the bosom or breast of God, not to mention putting God into a body that is commonly objectified, takes on sexual connotations. To set aside this image in favor of a more socially acceptable portrayal is problematic on several levels. First, the meaning conveyed in this picture of Jesus at the bosom of God is one of extraordinary tenderness. One would be hard-pressed to secure a description of a relationship more intimate than that of nursing a child. God is a life-sustainer in the Fourth Gospel, which is not a metaphorical platitude, but underscores the claim of the incarnation. If, at any time, "the Word made flesh" is simply a euphemism, then it ceases to be the doctrinal claim that we confess.

Second, at stake in this image is not only who Jesus is as the Word made flesh, as the unique and one and only God, but also who we are as believers. The only other time in the Gospel of John that the word *bosom* is used is in 13:23 (NKJV), the first introduction to the disciple whom Jesus loves. It is, at the very least, odd that this beloved disciple is never mentioned before this point in the story. Why is that? If Jesus loves this disciple so much, where has he been the first twelve chapters? The beloved disciple's introduction and placement in the story indicate that his function and meaning are more important than his identity. While scholars still devote significant effort to determining narratively and theologically who the beloved disciple was, the more important question is *why* the beloved disciple. The fact that the term *bosom* only occurs in 1:18 and 13:23 affirms the premise of John that every claim about the relationship between God and Jesus is, at the same time, a claim about the relationship between the believer and God/ Jesus. Describing the relationship between Jesus and God has little import if the believer is not able to imagine that same relationship personally and experientially with God and Jesus. This is the "why" of the beloved disciple—that we are able to imagine being nourished at the breast of God, just as Jesus himself knew and experienced. This connection between Jesus at the breast of God and the beloved disciple, the believer, at the breast of God underscores the nature of faith and belief; it begins with vulnerability and is experienced and grounded in it. The translation issues surrounding John 1:18 that do not make the connection to 13:23 reveal the discomfort in our church cultures with sexuality and vulnerability.

This rather brief biblical foray into John is meant to give imagination to what theological vulnerability actually means, and to serve as a reminder that it matters. God becomes human, God becomes a particular human, and according to John, God invites a relationship with God that is profoundly intimate, mutual, reciprocal, and vulnerable. This suggests that ministry is about revealing who God is and the relationship God wants, vulnerability included.

The use of the word *bosom* has profound implications for what it means to be a woman in ministry. This image, this language, this way of understanding our relationship with God is part of the fabric of faith, and of what the church is called to be. This is not simply a feminine image for God. This is describing what relationship with God is like and underscoring the inherent vulnerability of relationship that we would rather ignore. To be human is to be vulnerable. It is to be susceptible to physical, mental, and emotional harm or risk. To know the potential for harm is also to know the necessity of dependence. That is, susceptibility in turn demands dependence. The truth of a theology of vulnerability means that we embrace dependence—on each other and on God. Calling attention to this presentation of God is not to claim that women have a better hold on dependence, but to suggest that an image such as this, embodied in the bodies of women, can therefore be embodied in the women called to preach and teach the good news of God's love.

To have a starting point in ministry that takes this aspect of God seriously would reorient our inclinations away from relationships that are self-serving and hurtful. We would come from a place of kindness, realizing that we live in a vulnerable world. As a woman in ministry, part of your calling needs to be to tell the truth about ways of doing ministry that presume that hurtful approaches are acceptable. Why you? Because you are, and you remain, by virtue of your position, a target of that potential for harm. We have to call out when we experience harm, and that it is harmful to us and to the church when our call is assumed to be less than acceptable to some, or even to God.

THE FEAR OF VULNERABILITY

The truth about ministry, regardless of gender, is that it is one of the most vulnerable vocations imaginable. It is radical exposure. There is really nowhere to hide. And yet so much of ministry makes every attempt to cover up our true selves, our hurt, our shame, our questions, and our uncertainties. Rather than vulnerability being perceived as a theological characteristic of God, it is perceived as an ecclesial liability. It seems that there is no other way to survive in ministry but to mask who you are.

How has this and does this continue to play out? Perceptions of persons in ministry still coalesce around assumptions that we have all the answers; that we are certain of our faith without ever having doubts; that we are capable at and even excel in all aspects of ministry, a "Jane-of-all-trades"; and that we are not susceptible to the basic common denominators of humanity largely described as sin, but more concretized by concepts like greed, lust, addiction, depression, and the like. The perceived pedestal on which persons in ministry are perched is very much still present in the church—even more so for women.

While your failings and fallouts might be common to all of humanity, they will be connected with your gender in ways that men in ministry will not experience. One pastor shared,

> In being farewelled from my parish yesterday, every comment I had from parishioners about why they would miss me was to do with my gender, appearance, age, or singing voice. The only person who mentioned my ministry was a newcomer who thanked me for welcoming them. So much for all those hours writing cutting edge sermons! So much for spiritual leadership! And to rub salt in the wound, for the 2nd time I was told how much I reminded them of Liesl from the Sound of Music (the most air-headed 16 year old in cinematic history who actually sings a song about needing an older male to tell her what to do). All very depressing when you're a 39 year old with a Masters degree. It seems that in my three years of providing ministry for them I've provided nothing more than light entertainment.

While your successes may be equivalent to any person who has leadership training and skills, it will come as a surprise to many that a woman is so capable of leading a flock. Who knew? This is especially true for women in ministry because we remain in many instances an unknown category. The hard part about vulnerability is the tendency to conflate critique and judgment, which are two different things. We take appraisal of our ministry personally. We experience evaluations of our work as statements about our being. This is when it is important, both on your end and in the assessment of the valuation itself, to distinguish between critique and judgment. Critique is gathering information and coming to a conclusion. Judgment is usually not interested in fairness. You may be inclined to overcompensate in performance and productivity, not only for the sake of your own position but for the sake of women in ministry in general. Your own fear will be the hardest truth to utter. While it is not necessarily your responsibility to carry the weight of the success of all women in ministry on your shoulders, it still is, to some extent. It is your responsibility in that there has to be a fundamental commitment to solidarity. Yet, it is not, because each woman has to be responsible for her own successes and failures in ministry. This is a very vulnerable place to be.

Another vulnerable aspect inherent to ministry is that you are allowed into the vulnerability of others much faster than any other profession or relationship. While it may be argued that doctors (both physical and mental) and lawyers are also privy to the most vulnerable moments in our lives, it is the minister to whom all of that which encompasses our humanity is revealed: health, relationships, and faith. The more you listen and abide in these spaces of vulnerability, the more you begin to wonder, "When will they discover my own?"

Not only is ministry inherently vulnerable because you are continually at risk for others observing your perceived faults and the aspects of yourself you would rather not have people see, but because you will constantly be exposing your very theology. In your teaching, preaching, and pastoral care, you are revealing who you are as a theologian for all the world to see. What if they disagree with you? What if they do not like your theology? What if they leave the church because of you? These fears then get personalized—"they do not like me"—into a fear of rejection. This is vulnerability at its very core: the fear and then the knowledge and potential of rejection.

So to placate the dissenters and the disbelievers and so to not be rejected, we play it safe theologically. Rather than reveal what we truly think, we revert to the theological default button. Then, if someone does not agree with us, if someone does not like what we say, if someone leaves the church or abandons the relationship, we can safely say, "That's the official opinion of..." and insert our denomination, our church, our creeds, our confessions, or our loyalties.

This is one of the reasons why preaching right now is so incredibly boring. Preachers are unwilling to expose their own theological interpretation of a text, and so they quote commentaries, fall back to theological jargon, or hide behind generally acceptable sacramentology in order to avoid having to state their own theological truth. The flip side of the coin, however, is no more conducive to vulnerability, for there are those preachers whose proclamation is so definitive as not to allow any opportunity for wonder. This is because to reveal yourself, or to invite questions, creates vulnerable spaces that are hard to negotiate in the parish—and in life.

For a woman in ministry, preaching your vulnerable truth will be even harder. You will want to fall back on theological truths that feel more acceptable, more palatable, with the idea that you will have enough trouble as it is, without upsetting the theological apple cart. You will want to make sure that your theology is "correct" and sound; you will want to have all of your theological ducks in a row so as to be taken seriously and to get or keep a job when a congregation is reluctant to hire you. But who determines "theological correctness"?

Who has been allowed to determine theological correctness is exactly the point. Theological correctness has been avowed by a male-dominated tradition, which is, in part, why male truths/experiences feel less vulnerable in preaching and seem safer. Commentaries on the Bible and monographs in theology are predictable because they all emerge from one fairly uniform set of white, straight, cisgender[4] privileged experiences. Your theological abilities will perhaps be taken more seriously, or will at least have more integrity, if you are willing to challenge the usual, question the status quo, and speak up for those who have been theologically overlooked. Playing it safe theologically is not a biblical principle; it should not be a principle of your ministry either.

What is it about the church that makes it so incredibly nervous about vulnerability? What does it have to fear? In part it is because vulnerability is misunderstood by most, including the church. Equated with sharing too much or being weak, it is a characteristic that one would do best to avoid. The reality, however, as discussed above, is that our world and our lives are vulnerable places. Brené Brown defines vulnerability as uncertainty, risk, and emotional exposure.[5] If Brown is right, the institutional church cannot afford to lift up vulnerability as a valued characteristic of ministry. For much of its history, the church has enjoyed cultural, social, and worldly power. The loss of that power in recent years has led to a defensive posture rather than one open to adaptation, change, and risk. The instinct toward traditionalism, the insistence that there is a pure church to which to return, and the entrenchment of acceptable doctrine all arise from a fear of decline. The church as it is now, with systems in place committed to its survival, has adapted our societal expectations of success as strength and certainty. These systems include, but are not limited to, its pastoral hierarchies, its polity, its judicatories, and even its sacraments. If the church were to stand on a principle of vulnerability, all of the above would be called into question. Therefore, a stick-your-head-in-the-sand philosophy seems viable so as to avoid the hard work of change.

At the same time, this is the very reason that a theology of vulnerability needs to take center stage in how we are church and how we do church. To speak up for and do ministry from a position of vulnerability as a woman in ministry could very well be an act of prophecy—although we all know how prophets tend to be received. Once again, this is about truth-telling. When the women went to the disciples and told them the truth about the empty tomb, what was the reaction by those closest to Jesus throughout his ministry? That the truth-telling by the women was garbage or crap (*lēros*; Luke 24:11). Truth-telling is rarely received with acceptance, but it is absolutely necessary. The prophets knew this. Jesus knew this. The women at the tomb knew this. Truth-telling is the hallmark of the gospel. It makes the gospel be the gospel and it will make the church be church.

VULNERABILITY AND EMBODIMENT

Accepting and embracing vulnerability is also essential to unlocking our power as women in ministry because it has everything to do with our bodies and embodiment. While we can obscure our true selves and hide our theological commitments quite easily if we choose, our bodies are much harder to disguise, although we try desperately to do so. Our bodies are essential to and revealing of who we are. We express ourselves through our bodies, which communicate what we think and feel as much as our words do.

This is particularly true in ministry. Ministry does not happen solely through speech, but through action, through our bodies acting out our theological commitments. Ministry is about bodies touching bodies—in sharing the peace, in praying, in baptisms, in Holy Communion, in pastoral care, and in commendation of the dying. This is also life, of course. But in life and especially in ministry, we need to be much more conscious of the kinds of effects our bodies have on others, both for good and for ill. Bodies express intimacy, which is essential to relationship but can also destroy it. Intimacy is all too often misinterpreted or abused; misconstrued relationships can result in sexual and ethical harassment and violation. We know that there are many persons in our lives, directly and indirectly, who seem unaware of how their bodies communicate with and affect those around them. For ministry, since the body is connected to acts carried out in the name of God, the stakes are higher. Ministry has to reflect a theology of embodiment.

One example of how critical it is to think about the body and its role in the call to ministry is in the task of preaching. Preaching is possibly the most public act of theology when it comes to ministry. It is also an act of extraordinary power, a kind of power that has to be assessed carefully. For many of the reasons outlined in our discussion about KEY NUMBER ONE, the preacher is afforded an authority rather unprecedented in other arenas of life. While authority, and its accompanying figures, continues to be a location of societal critique, a preacher still has attributed authority, in part because of the nature of the subject matter on which she preaches.

A preacher is afforded an assumed authority because she is preaching the gospel, the scriptures, the Word of God (note capitalization).

But preaching is not just about the words that one speaks. As a result, one's body is connected with that power and authority of which the preacher must constantly be aware. Our bodies have the potential to comfort and console, to nurture and to protect, but also the possibility of wielding power that brings about pain, suffering, and even death. Bodies that tower, bodies that yell, bodies that shake their fists and point and pin down, are not those that seek to present an interpretive point but those that intend to coerce and subjugate into belief. A preacher has to consider what, and how, her body is communicating, with as much care as she considers her words and her tone. Preaching is not simply about content, but about embodied content. Preaching is a necessary act for understanding the theological promise of the incarnation. The Word becomes flesh again in proclamation, incarnated anew in the body of the preacher and in the body of the congregation. To take the incarnation seriously means that we have to take our bodies seriously.

In the act of preaching, the consciousness of our bodies works itself out in a number of ways. Because of the versatility of our bodies and our gestures, they are a medium for intimating emotion. Our bodies can actually work against our words, with an ill-placed or ill-timed gesture, or a bodily stance that contradicts what we are saying. At the same time, our bodies can be used to enhance our communication in ways that only using words cannot. It is never just what you say, but always how you say it, and a major mode of our communication is our bodies.

Yet, there are too many voices out there, voices that are usually far too loud and too influential, that continue to insist, especially to beginning preachers, that words are enough and that the body can only be a distraction from the very important act of proclaiming God's word. Their advice is usually something along the lines of "you need to get out of the way of the gospel" or "get yourself out of the way so that the word of God can be heard." Sometimes this ill-informed advice refers to the need for preachers to be aware of their own issues and not have too much of themselves in a sermon, whether in stories or illustrations about themselves, their opinions, the proverbial soapbox, or even their theological ideas.

For all these reasons of self-awareness, it is essential to know yourself as a biblical interpreter and as a theologian. But this kind of advice betrays the assumption that the word of God can be communicated without the subjectivity of the preacher. We have already chronicled in the discussion about KEY NUMBER ONE that objectivity when it comes to biblical interpretation and theological thinking is an impossibility, which, in fact, makes a dangerous claim about the authority of scripture. The Word of God was incarnated, embodied in the man named Jesus and lived in Jesus's ministry, touching on all human senses and experience. God's word, then, must also be experienced—felt, seen, tasted, smelled, and yes, heard. It takes the body, and relationships between bodies that are mutual and interdependent, to make that happen.

Bodies are incredibly vulnerable things on multiple levels, and how women feel about their bodies is perhaps the most acute sensation of vulnerability that we experience in our lives. We are all too aware of the attention that is given to women's bodies—on all levels. Lest we think the obsession with the bodies of straight women is the only point of interest, we need only to consider the fixation on lesbian bodies in terms of sex and "how does that work?" or trans women with regard to genitalia, hormones, and surgery to recognize that no woman is safe from inspection and objectification. We are also exceedingly aware of the attention we give to our own bodies. Why do we need to talk about our bodies so much as women in ministry? Because everyone else does and everyone else will.

Bodies are complicated because they are intimately connected to how we, in general, feel about ourselves: our confidence, certainly, but also our feelings of inadequacy and whether or not we see ourselves as worthy of love and affection. Our perception of our bodies is already predisposed to shame and criticism. Bodies, then, are especially complicated as women in ministry because feelings of inadequacy in our ministry will then be felt bodily—in our bodies and because of our bodies.

The obsession with the female body in our time and culture needs little proof; our experience of it needs no defense. We know this truth and we are fully aware of its consequences in our society and in our world. At the same time, this obsession cannot be set aside with the willfully blind insistence that it does not make a difference for how you do ministry or how you feel about yourself. Especially as a woman, your body will be linked with how do you ministry; what then has the potential to surface are feelings about your body, both negative and positive, that you never knew you had.

We know that the perceptions of and ideals for the female body are both unrealistic and unrealizable for straight women but all the more for those who are gender-fluid or queer. Yet, this awareness does little to eliminate the irrationality. We can tell ourselves endlessly that the bodies we see on television, in movies, and in advertisements are impossibilities; that it is part of their vocation to look like they do; that they have personal trainers, personal chefs, and the financial resources for anything and everything from skincare to plastic surgery in order to achieve "perfection"; that, in fact, these bodies are not even real after editing and airbrushing; but if we are honest, none of that really makes any difference. We still judge and evaluate our own bodies as imperfect at best, repulsive and justifiably rejected at worst. Self-judgment is no more potent and powerful than when we are forced to offer an evaluation of our bodies. And as much as we disdain being objects of desire, deep down in places we rarely let anyone see, we want to be wanted because being wanted is connected to worth and belonging.

We tell ourselves, "I am more than my body," and we are, but only so much self-talk can convince us of that truth. We tell ourselves that our bodies are as unique as the souls that inhabit them. We tell ourselves, "This is the body God has given me." We tell ourselves that we just have to do better about being comfortable in our own skin. But no amount of self-talk can overcome those many moments when, as a woman in ministry, it is your very body that will be rejected—every curve, every angle; your waist, your breasts; your height and your weight. People will notice and comment on every change in your body and any change you make to your body. And your body will likely be connected to your perceived abilities for ministry. One pastor shared that one response in a performance review was, "She excels in every way except that she is overweight."

We might even offer theological rationale for uniqueness of our bodies, that women are made in the image of God just as much as men. But if you rarely, if ever, hear about God's femininity, female images for God, or female characteristics of God, then even that biblical truth will be hard to believe. If God is mostly assumed to be male, referred to with male pronouns, and described as male, then it will be more difficult and take more energy to imagine God in female categories. This will take a lot of theological effort and again why a biblical imagination for how you think of ministry and do ministry is essential.

We also know that for many women, the dominant reference to God as Father, and the fact that Jesus is male, have proven very difficult, to the point of being a reason to reject faith altogether. If we enter into ministry ignorant of these experiences, we do so at our own peril, assuming aspects of God that we ourselves are upending by our very embodied presence.

To live into your full power as a woman in ministry means that you have to figure out what you are going to do with your body. Do you feel comfortable in your own skin? This starts with being honest with your personal feelings about your own body—whether you like it or not; what parts you do like and do not like; how you let it be seen and how you conceal it. This will take some historical work as well. How has your relationship with your body changed over the years because of age, health, pregnancy, or simply life passages? Do you celebrate your femininity or disguise it? For that matter, what does femininity mean to you? Is it important to you or not? Have you ever felt like your body has betrayed you, that it has let you down? Have you experienced times when your body was ridiculed or criticized? Has your body been abused or been used in the context of emotional or psychological abuse? This will be exceedingly difficult self-reflection, yet it is essential for embodying the truth of your ministry.

This may not be work you can do alone. You may need a partner, a friend, or a therapist to offer some objectivity because our ability to see what is true is compromised, even when we literally look into the mirror, because of how we internalize how our bodies are perceived by most.

BODIES AND EMBODIMENT

The thing that is really hard, and really amazing, is giving up on being perfect and beginning the work of becoming yourself.

—*Anna Quindlen*

A significant factor that further complicates our relationship with our bodies as women in ministry is what to wear. While we will address attire in more depth in chapter 4, we will point out here all the ways in which women use clerical garb (albs, clergy shirts, robes, and cassocks, if clergy) to exercise some control over how people view their bodies. For example, there are clergywomen who do not use a cincture, or rope, when wearing an alb so as not to accentuate the fact that they have a waist, hips, and breasts. There are female clergy who have been told that their choice of alb, especially clergy attire specifically designed for women's bodies, is too form-fitting or too tailored. Of course, the description "form-fitting" means that it fits her body well; that it conforms to the outline of her body in such a way that you can see it is her body—that you can see it is a woman's body. The comment is not a "meant to be helpful" or benign comment about appropriate clergy dress. The comment is a blatant disclosure either of the person's discomfort with the female body or perception of it as distracting. One pastor noted, "I do have a problem with comments on wardrobe if they are truly sexist, and the 'more tailored dress' comment certainly is because it clearly relates professionalism to a more masculine style." To be a sexual being is not the same as "using" your sexuality, yet this is the operating assumption. If you are perceived as comfortable in yourself as a sexual being, then that must mean some sort of attempt to play your sexuality for some gain. Comments like that also communicate our cultural predilection for victim-blaming: "if you wear that, then all I can think about is that you are an object of sexual desire, and it's distracting to think that about my pastor," which puts the blame for their discomfort squarely upon you. The church is not immune to rape culture (see sexism glossary in chapter 4). In fact, it is a bastion of it.

This, then, leads to an important truth about being a woman in ministry, about having a leadership role in the church: no matter what it says, the church is not ready for you. In fact, not only is the church (including its seminaries, its judicatories, and its governances) not ready for you, but it will continue persistently, systematically, and even systemically to resist and reject placing women in ministry, particularly in roles with power—especially women who conform most to the cultural ideals of feminine desirability. At the same time, while it is true that the more you represent the "ideal" woman, the less likely you will be able to advance in ministry or hold positions that are more public or perceived as having more authority, if you are gender-fluid or ambiguous, it will hurt you just as badly. Being a woman in ministry does not release you from being considered and viewed as a sexual object. The dominant attitude seems to be that women can be in ministry as long as they do not conform to our cultural norms of beauty and sexuality. Women can be seen as having power and possessing leadership skills, until they are identified as an object of sexual desire, and then that is a far too uncomfortable scenario.

As a result, one tactic women in ministry employ to navigate this truth is to downplay their femininity. How you choose to express your femininity or gender identity should be your choice, yet many women feel as if the choice has been made for them. This is all the more complex when we understand the ways in which femininity gets defined. While femininity is most often thought of as having to do with the nature of the female sex, that definition depends on gender binary. Consider this definition from the Gender and Sexuality Center at the University of Texas at Austin: "Femininity is a gender identity constructed socially, historically, and politically. It is the cultural interpretation of femaleness, learned through participation in society and its institutions. Femininity can be seen as a form of ideology, in that it presents a set of cultural ideals that define appropriate roles, values, and expectations for and of women."[6]

In order to advance in the church, in order to be considered for positions of power, positions that put you forward as the face of the church, women in ministry are tacitly informed that femininity must be set aside for a more "professional" look. How you choose to express your gender identity should not be an issue, but it is. This is not at all to suggest that women in ministry should look a certain way or strive toward an expectation of femininity determined by others in order to fulfill their call; rather, it is to say that each woman should be able to embody what it means to be a woman in her own way, without it affecting her career.

How you embody who are as a woman has everything to do with how your power will be perceived. The effectiveness of one's power is associated with one's authenticity and one's truth. How your power is appreciated and interpreted will be directly connected to whether people witness your true self, or some inauthentic "acceptable" version of yourself, based on what you think they want or expect to see. This is not unlike the correlation people witness between pastor and preacher: who you are as the one who leads Bible study, who prays at council meetings, and who visits in hospital rooms has to be the same person who preaches God's word from the pulpit. If there is a disconnect between the preaching pastor and the everyday pastor, both venues give rise to suspicion—who is the true person I call pastor? One's credibility and believability is called into question. It will also be the object of your ministry, which we will discuss in more detail in the chapter on sexism.

BODIES AND CHANGE

Pregnancy should be a celebratory moment when it comes to women's bodies, yet is one of the most challenging and troubling issues connected with the female body, particularly in ministry. If you become pregnant while serving in a church, expect that comments about your body will abound. After a Good Friday service, one pastor, six months pregnant at the time, had a female member approach her and say, "Listen, we were talking about it, and your boobs are getting HUGE!" There will be opinions about your choice of maternity clothes, either voiced or not, and people will view your baby as theirs even before it is born, and so therefore feel proprietary about the way you are caring for your own body. There will be many men, and a few women, in your church who simply will not know what to do with or how to handle your pregnancy. There is something extraordinarily powerful and threatening about a pregnant woman. Whether it is your ability to give birth; to give life; to handle the physical challenges and changes; or whether it is the fact that there is nothing a man can do to secure the birth of his child, and there is, therefore a realization of a lack of control, a pregnant woman is intimidating. In part, this discomfort is connected to your changing body. Your body was hard enough to handle as simply female, and now maternity imparts changes that accentuate what makes female bodies worrisome and threatening in the first place. It is likely that the increased size of your breasts alone will be difficult for many.

It is one thing to witness these bodily changes in a friend or family member but quite another thing to witness them in your pastor. With pregnancy comes the disquieting reminder that your pastor is a sexual being. While we can usually push that truth aside for the most part, pretending that your pastor does not have sex, this truth is front and center if you become pregnant. Even in situations where there has been assisted reproduction, pregnancy equals sex. The discomfort with a pregnant pastor, therefore, lies not only in response to changes in your body, but in the realization that your pastor has sex and even has an active sex life. Men, although we should not presuppose heterosexuality here, are far more prone to this experience, and they can only wonder, question, even fantasize about your sexuality. They have thought about how often you have sex and whether or not you like it. They have likely thought about having sex with you. Yet on a daily basis, most of these thoughts can be compartmentalized or pushed aside. This is not the case when you are pregnant because of the obvious thought (unless you have been open about medical intervention for infertility, and sometimes even then) that to become pregnant you would have had to have sex. Now the thoughts that could be abated about your sexuality and your sexual patterns are much harder to ignore.

The enhanced vulnerability of your body during pregnancy is important to anticipate. Our self-consciousness about our bodies is heightened, as is our anxiety about our bodies that are no longer within our control. If we wonder what people think of our bodies when we are not pregnant, imagine that feeling increasing exponentially when we are. Expect comments about your weight, regardless if you are pregnant or not. If your weight is something about which you are sensitive, you will need to think about how to handle these comments. One pastor shared the story of a woman saying to her, when the pastor was about five months pregnant, "So are you going to lose all the weight by February?" The pastor responded, "No, I'm having a baby in February, so I'll keep getting bigger until then." Furthermore, if your instinct has been to hide your body, you will not be able to do so when you are pregnant. You will need to be prepared for what that exposure will feel like and how you will cope with it. The increased vulnerability that comes with pregnancy also exists in the assumption that your body, particularly your belly, is now available for the entire world to touch. If you have insecurity about your body to begin with, the thought of it being touched by people with whom you are not necessarily close will be terrifying. There will be people who will ask first, but more often than not, people presume that your body is now a public space because of your pregnancy. You will need to anticipate how you will handle these advances and how you will cope with the after effects. Touch is a profoundly intimate sense. How we adjudicate touch signals comfort and discomfort with our bodies and communicates both past histories and present circumstances about our relationship with our bodies.

CLOTHING, MAKEUP, AND WHAT NOT TO WEAR

This section begins with a simple statement: what not to wear is anything that does not reflect who you are. Yet, at the same time, what you wear in ministry quickly becomes who you are. That is, your clothing, makeup, jewelry, and shoes suddenly become the objects of everyone's interest as a woman in ministry and will get far more attention and many more comments than your theological or ministerial gifts and capabilities. You will soon begin to wonder if there is anything else people see in you besides what you look like. The honest answer is not much. Your appearance will be that by which your performance is assessed. As one pastor noted, "I have no problem with people commenting on my wardrobe in a casual 'I love your jacket' kind of way. As long as the comment isn't sexual, and as long as my performance isn't evaluated based on my style." Be prepared for your wardrobe to be more interesting than your ministry or your merits. This phenomenon is frequently more present in the early months of your call, in part because people have not had a chance to get to know you. They scramble for something complimentary to say, theoretically to build a relationship with you, yet the default comments will hinge on how you look. While these observations can be attenuated over time and relationship building, they are nonetheless difficult to hear when you are longing for respect with regard to your ministry itself. The additional challenge is to know when to respond to the shockingly inappropriate comments.

For clergy, to wear or not wear a robe and a clerical collar is the first wardrobe decision. As one pastor notes, "I always wanted to wear a robe because then people might be paying attention to what I was saying rather than what I was (or was not) wearing." Wearing a clerical collar brings immediate recognition, but it will also be the cause of surprise and a variety of perplexed reactions. It will communicate your position and authority, but it will also invite wonder, likely conversation, yet sometimes even hateful reactions. One pastor shared, "A woman in my apartment complex shouted at me when I was wearing my collar on my way to my car, 'You're a whore, you're disgusting, get away in Jesus' name.'" This pastor then went on, "Granted, she is not all mentally there, but her words sank deep into the wound that festers when I hear echoes of 'You are crazy to believe that God would choose you, that God would say yes to you.'"

Clothing has everything to do with embodiment and what it means to be embodied, what incarnated ministry looks like. Your clothing is critical to your ministry, not because you have to have the perfect outfit or always look stunning, but because it will be so wrongly connected to how you do ministry. You will have to acknowledge this reality. Acknowledgment does not assume acceptance but savvy. It is to be fully aware that both men and women will comment on your appearance: men, because they usually do not know what else to say to a woman who is given more power than they and so the instinctual move is to objectify them; women, because they see you as competition and because women are conditioned to comment upon one another's appearance from a very young age.

Clothing, while a mode of protection, also creates the potential for fear. What you choose to wear has the possibility of procuring unwanted advances because, of course, if you wear that kind of clothing, our culture of victim blaming assumes that you want those kinds of advances. It will likely be the cause of the most friction from or difficult relationships with the women in your congregation. They will compare themselves to you, perhaps even want to look like you and be like you, because they see in you power that they do not have.

People have certain ideas of what a minister should look like, as discussed above, but also when it comes to women in ministry, what is deemed "appropriate" for them to wear: "The minister should not wear that," or "I never thought a minister could look so sexy/hot," which would never be said to any of your male colleagues. The truth is, you will simply not believe what people are capable of saying. Other pastors shared the following stories:

One pastor was told repeatedly that she "didn't dress in a feminine enough manner."

"Parishioners brought clothes for me to try on, blouses which they said would be better suited to my role than the blouses I wore."

"I often receive negative comments from the (generally) older population about wearing pants instead of skirts, about my nail polish colors, and my hairstyle. And also commenting that I walk too much like a man (but they think it's probably OK because I'm the pastor)."

"At my second local ministerium meeting (with all UCC pastors), an older male pastor came up to me and said, 'Well, you look much more like a pastor this time.' The first meeting I had worn jeans and a nice top. The second meeting I wore a dress and blazer."

In the receiving line, a pastor was told that "my grandson and I really, really like having a sexy pastor."

"I once had a visiting soloist at my first solo call who came up to me before worship looking astonished. 'YOU'RE the pastor?!' she exclaimed loudly. When I politely replied, 'Yes, I'm Pastor Heidi, it's nice to meet you,' she responded, 'But ministers aren't usually so pretty!'"

"One woman said during the children's sermon, as an aside, 'I know a name for women who wear shoes like that. But I won't say it in church.' (I was wearing high heels.)"

All of this is complicated by the ability to parse the real issue behind the comment. Is it a matter of professional attire or is the underlying problem with a woman in ministry? Your wardrobe is fair game for any and all comments either positive or negative. Rarely, if ever, is this a concern for a man in ministry. In fact, your male colleagues are able to get away with all kinds of wardrobe missteps and malfunctions that you will never be able to. They will rarely, if ever, receive comments on their clothing.

A first reaction to this truth is one of anger. How can this be? How can this *still* be? As long as I do my job well, why should anyone care what I wear? And we should be angry, very angry, because clothing is just one example of the double standards that exist for women in ministry. "I was critiqued in the church in ways that no employer would ever critique my wardrobe," said one pastor. Another pastor was told she needed to look more "professional." But what does "professional" mean if not still alluding to male garb? One pastor's response to the meaning of "professional" was the following: "For women, it is an essentially useless, loaded term which means walking the impossible line between not-male and not-distractingly/desirably female. So: skirts, but not too short; heels, but not too high; color, but not too bright. It is a constant reminder that we still live in a patriarchal culture that makes men the subjects and women the objects."

A second response, however, can be strategy and opportunity—what you wear can indeed be one way to exercise and communicate your power as a woman in ministry. Because if what you wear is truly indicative of who you are, the unspoken truth in the comments that are made is that others see an integrated self: that what they see is also who they know.

The first strategy for navigating what to wear as a woman in ministry is to know what you feel comfortable wearing and what is an expression of yourself. Your clothing should be a reflection of who you are because it communicates much about you. It tells people if you care about fashion and style. It communicates your level of comfort with your body—whether you let others see it or whether you do everything you can to hide it. It communicates how much you are aware of your own body, what looks good on it and what doesn't. Your clothing reflects your comfort, or lack thereof, with your own sexuality. It tells others whether or not clothing is important to you and how much time you think about it. Your clothing says something about how you choose to negotiate your femininity, what femininity means to you, and in what ways it is an expression of your gender identity. Whether you embrace it, reject it, or find yourself somewhere in between, nonetheless what you wear intimates your feelings about femininity.

In the end, since your clothing is a reflection of who you are, it has to be authentic to you and fit your body. Not only do we hide our bodies behind our clothing, we hide our very selves behind our clothing. We hope that our clothing can deflect the ability of people to see who we really are. We do not want to be seen, lest our faults and our mistakes be seen as well. But if our clothing is unworthy of mention, we are also communicating to some extent that we are unworthy of being noticed. Rather than provide protection from being seen, our clothing suggests that there is something wrong to be seen.

You have likely been a witness to situations where it is clear that a woman has been given some direction in what to wear. Something has been said to her, that she needs to update her wardrobe, she needs to look more "something," which could include feminine, professional, presidential, ministerial, businesslike, and so on. Yet dressing to fit the tastes and desires of someone other than yourself will tend less to improve your appearance than to work against you because it frequently becomes obvious you have been asked to wear certain clothes, jewelry, and makeup that are counter to who you know yourself to be. You feel uncomfortable and you look uncomfortable because rather than being an indication of who you are, your clothing is a likeness of what someone thinks you should be. This inauthenticity will not pass unnoticed and will arouse more suspicion than reassurance. Your clothing has to reflect your identity, your sense of agency, rather than the objectification that others would impose.

Your clothing, hairstyle, and makeup are usually the first things that people will notice. People will observe immediately if you have done something different to your hair, and they will comment on the change. Short of a drastic alteration, this will not be true of your male colleagues. Of course, it tends to be a given that men change their hair far more infrequently than women. Yet, just because women tend to do more with their hair than men does not have to mean that it has to be a constant topic of conversation—but it will be. Another popular topic of conversation will be your makeup—whether or not you wear it, whether you wear too much or too little, how you apply it, and so on.

Comments about your hairstyle and makeup are not simply superficial comments, but are implicated when it comes to assessing your leadership. Furthermore, they are assessed based on standards that usually have more to do with societal expectations about beauty rather than any particular standards associated with professionalism or leadership. It is, of course, the latter set of standards that women in ministry should care about when it comes to how they are perceived. However, it is difficult, if not impossible, to ignore the cultural values set out for how we portray ourselves to the world. Our looks are appreciated not for how they might be representative of who we are but for how they are computed in comparison to standards of beauty outside of our own sense of being, truth, and worth.

This becomes the most difficult reality to traverse when you receive comments and compliments about your hair, makeup, and clothing— that the measurement in place has nothing to do with what is truly you, but with what our culture has deemed "acceptable" beauty. The litmus test for appearance is not determined by how it best represents our true selves, but by how it best epitomizes, even symbolizes, the ideal of female desirability. For this reason alone, how you choose to style your hair and how you decide what and how much makeup to wear has to be a reflection of your own identity, your own self. That it is a reflection of your identity may be something only you and those closest to you will know, but at least you know it and believe it, whether or not most everybody else realizes it. For the most part, knowing this will make the comments easier to tolerate.

This is not what we want, necessarily; it is not what we would hope, but it is the truth. Clothing has everything to do with first impressions, and as a leader, first impressions matter. They really do. And here is the double standard: you cannot expect to be thought of as a leader if you do not look like one, but how you look will garner far more scrutiny than your male colleagues will experience. Men in ministry can get away with looking like slobs. They can truly wear whatever they want and receive few if any comments about what they wear and what they look like. If they do get comments on their less-than-appropriate pastoral attire, it will be something along the lines of "Oh, that's just Pastor Mike." In other words, no matter what he looks like or what he wears, it is recognized as being a reflection of who he is. At the same time, we have to be intentional about what we look like in order for it to be considered a reflection of who we are. We can put this phenomenon, like many issues discussed in this book, in the category of "crap men don't have to think about." They do not have to think about what they wear, even when it is obvious that they should.

The amount of frustration and even infuriation caused by the seem-ingly endless interest in and comments about how you look is nothing short of overwhelming. An important but sobering exercise is to keep a log of the comments that you receive in a week. Like the sexism log that will be suggested in KEY NUMBER FOUR, keeping a log of comments about your appearance will allow you to make note of just how perva-sive these comments truly are. What will be important to expect, how-ever, is that these comments will come from both men and women, each with their own motivations and meanings. As discussed above, and what will be discussed further in KEY NUMBER FOUR, the range that these comments represent is vast: from the actually complimentary to well-meaning and admiring, to unwitting sexism and deliberate sexism, to bla-tant sexual desire, and all the way to intentional verbiage to undermine your power and confidence. From women, the range is equally extensive: from complimentary and sincerely interested, to solidarity (because there are professional women in our churches who have to deal with this reality as well), to competition, jealousy, and envy.

Recognizing the commonality and consistency of these comments helps you realize—even believe—that you are not making this up and that this double standard is truly happening. The log will also help you document these instances for what they are: observations about your appearance, not comments about your ministry. It can also be a relief to your frustrated feelings when you understand that you are not going crazy—and then you can let it go. You are more than how you look and what you wear; we know this, but we all need to be reminded of this truth from time to time.

How we cope with the feeling that others assess our ministry by what we wear and how we look is of vital importance. You can choose not to pay attention to it and decide that you are not going to give in to this double standard, but then you will need to be aware of the upshots of this decision. This is not fair, of course. For women, what we wear and how we look will be critiqued regardless of whether or not it is a reflection of who we are. The consequences will be that how you look will be a constant state of affairs, if how you look is perceived as a direct affront to the office you hold. That is, one of the unspoken issues about what you wear and how you look is that you represent not only yourself but also your congregation or ministry setting. This matters for the people you serve. Much of this depends on the demographics of your parish, but more often than not, you are the primary symbol bearer of that congregation to the outside community. A congregation does not want to be in a situation where it has to defend you because this means defending their church and its ministry simultaneously. In other words, an important aspect of what you wear and how you look is respect: respect for the office, respect for yourself, respect for the congregation and the community it serves. While it is likely that a male in ministry will have to think even minimally about this, women will have to be aware of this constantly. The truth is also that a man in ministry will not garner this same kind of attention because he already embodies the paradigm in place. No one would dare comment on his looks with the intention of suggesting a makeover, but they will for you.

What you wear and how you look are not simply choices you make for your own sake, but choices that communicate to your church and to your community who you know yourself to be. When these choices are consistently questioned, the inevitable result can be a constant state of heightened vulnerability. The first strategy in dealing with this kind of overexposure is to expect it, rather than pretending or hoping that it will not happen to you.

CLOSING THOUGHTS

Telling the truth about vulnerability, bodies, and sexuality may very well be the most difficult truth we tell. The admission of vulnerability is risky and it seems that ministry already comes with enough risk and we do not really need any more. But that is the truth that God tells. Inherent to God is vulnerability and risk, and so our way of doing ministry has to be an expression of that theological claim. If we steer clear of vulnerability and embodiment, we embrace only God's divinity. God counts on us, God needs us, to do ministry in such a way that tells the whole truth of God.

EXERCISES AND QUESTIONS FOR REFLECTION

1. Be honest. How do you feel about your body? What parts do you like/dislike?

2. When has your body been critiqued or ridiculed? What was the circumstance?

3. When do you feel the most comfortable in your body and why?

4. What do you think your body communicates about you?

RESOURCES

http://beautytipsforministers.com.

Brené Brown, *Daring Greatly: How the Courage to Be Vulnerable Transforms the Way We Live, Love, Parent, and Lead* (New York: Avery, 2012).

———. "The Power of Vulnerability," TED.com, June 2010, http://www.ted.com/talks/brene_brown_on_vulnerability?language=en.

Melissa Lynn DeRosia, Marianne J. Grano, Amy Morgan, and Amanda Adams Riley, *The Girlfriends' Clergy Companion: Surviving and Thriving in Ministry* (Herndon, VA: Alban Institute, 2011).

Elizabeth Hayt, "Women of Which Cloth? Tweed? Cashmere?" *New York Times*, March 28, 1999, http://www.nytimes.com/1999/03/28/style/women-of-which-cloth-tweed-cashmere.html?pagewanted=1.

Sarah Sentilles, *A Church of Her Own: What Happens When a Woman Takes the Pulpit* (Orlando: Harcourt, 2008).

KEY NUMBER THREE

THE TRUTH ABOUT GENDER, IDENTITY, AND AUTHENTICITY

a bumble bee flies into my apartment
it didn't mean to be there—it panics
and seeing the outside through a glass window
it proceeds to push and push against the glass
trying to get where it wants to go
in its panic never moving from its task long enough
to see the open window just inches away
how like the bumble bee I am in my work or my life
i see where i want to go
and in my panic
i forget to look for the open window
so i push and push and push
thinking i should be rewarded for all this hard work
when, in fact, i am so frantic
like the bee against the glass.
—Marybeth Fidler, "The Bumble Bee"[1]

INTRODUCTION

KEY NUMBER THREE for unlocking the power of women in ministry is to embrace the necessity that your ministry be authentic to who you are.

In general, there will not be major resistance to the concept of authenticity in your ministry. In fact, authenticity seems rather in vogue today—be your true self, live out of your truth—as if none of us had been authentic before. But the truth is, while there will not be active opposition to the *idea* of being your authentic self in ministry, living it out will be one of the hardest things you do and will be the actual point of objection. Often the primary obstacle to unlocking your power for ministry is your own self. That is, the need to trust in our true selves is frequently tied up with and determined by the person we want others to see.

What is authenticity? One way to think about authenticity is living life from the inside out, not the outside in. There are and there will continue to be pressures toward conformity. Authenticity is awareness; it is living life fully awake, knowing what your needs are and resisting toeing the line if your needs are discounted. Authenticity does not preclude being a jerk. You can be authentically a jerk or authentically a lovely person. Authenticity does not guarantee a leader who leads for the sake of the good of the other. Rather, authenticity has to do with a level of trust, that the person before you is truly the person he or she is; that there is a correlation between demonstrated behavior/action and what's at stake for a person or to that person's commitments. Authenticity has to do with the fact that what you say and what you do are not separate from who you are. Your words and your actions are indeed windows through which to view your soul.

Jesus knew this well (Mark 7; cf. James 1; Psalm 15). Those who think they can convince others of their ideas as separate from their true selves are delusional. Authenticity is a biblical concept. If you expect to follow Jesus, then this will demand an excruciating examination of yourself, your true intentions, your true beliefs, and on what you stake your relationship with God. "Those who hear but don't do the word are like those who look at their faces in a mirror. They look at themselves, walk away, and immediately forget what they were like" (James 1:23-24). We might imagine some version of a pithy quote summarizing this verse from James on plaques and bumper stickers instead of self-righteous claims toward good works and quick judgments that are ignorant of the souls they reveal.

Authenticity in ministry is critical, but especially so for women in ministry for two reasons. First, as a woman in ministry, you already break the mold of what has been deemed authentic ministry. Authentic ministry has been male. Anything outside of that supposed authentic representation of ministry is cause for suspicion and will continue to be. Your ability to lead from your authentic self begins to erode some of this distrust. In part, this is about your character. For the most part, people want to believe you and they want to trust you. But if there is any sense that your authenticity could be called into question, the ramifications for you are far more detrimental than those of your male colleagues. Why? Because your authenticity as women in ministry is already put on alert because it does not conform to the status quo.

Second, how you maneuver the expectations of and claims about your ministry will depend on how you assess the authenticity of others. So many of those who think that their words and actions are worthy of our praise do not understand that it is their character we reject. Yet, at the same time, we spend a lot of energy saving, redeeming, and lifting up persons whose words and actions damage, demoralize, and demean. We posit, "They didn't really mean it. They didn't know what they were saying." Well, they probably did, and it is likely who they truly are. You can only tell the truth and be heard if you tell the truth of who you are. It is difficult but essential to live what we believe, to speak our truth, to be willing to bring forth in our words and our actions what is in our hearts. Those who are allowed to have a public hearing need also to accept the accountability and responsibility that comes along with such privilege.

This chapter begins with situating KEY NUMBER THREE within a biblical and theological framework. This chapter will also address issues for women in ministry that are directly connected to gender. Under gender, we will also discuss the concept of balance, and the specific challenges connected to balance when it comes to being a woman in ministry. Furthermore, authenticity is purposefully tied to gender because of specific challenges that you will face in how to live and work out of your authentic self.

Authenticity tends to be associated with and tied up in expectations of gender. That is, what is culturally and socially assumed about how women should act and be is then used to determine whether or not women are representing their true selves. It is most certainly a catch-22, when women try to live out of their authentic selves only to be told that they are not being the kind of women that society expects, wants, or deems appropriate. But authenticity is when your life is lived expressing your passions and your soul gifts.

Important in any discussion about gender is to recognize that gender identity and gender construction is far more complicated than most will assume, and certainly is more complicated than the church is usually willing to admit. This is particularly true for transgender or gender non-conforming persons who must not only negotiate their own gender identity with few resources and minimal support, but must also cope with gender expectations that do not fit their own struggles. Expectations of the incorrect gender are imposed upon certain people, which exacerbates the difficulty of living authentically. Being a woman in ministry calls forth sensitivity to these realities, to the ways in which our gender is continually denigrated, and to the ways in which this denigration is exacerbated for our sisters who struggle with gender identification.

BIBLICAL THEOLOGICAL COMPONENT

A biblical or theological basis for this chapter is harder to access because the Bible is not terribly interested, if at all, in our twenty-first-century issues around gender, identity, and authenticity. Placing modern psychological theory on the Bible, which is interpreting biblical characters through the lens of psychological development, is as unfair to scripture as taking its writings and words out of context.

At the same time, a biblical context for understanding our authentic selves—gender identity included—is essential because to unlock the power of being a woman in ministry means taking the roots, the beginnings of your vocation, seriously. It means seeing that you are entering into a long line of persons called to ministry, a line that began with the biblical witness. If your only recourse to being your authentic self in ministry is contemporary books on self-identity, then ministry becomes no different than any other profession.

Why is this so important for being a woman in ministry? Because people will see in you a resource for the construction of their own identities. You have to model what this looks like. There is no shortage of influences that compete for our attention, insisting that they can help to shape our individual identities, to live into our authentic selves. But you are not Oprah. You are a minister in, and for the sake of, God's kingdom. If you cannot articulate the difference for yourself, then there is no reason why you should imagine people will come to church and expect that the church will help them figure out and live into their identity. They have plenty of other means to do so and will find those means unless the church, and you, can speak meaningfully to their lives.

Unlocking your power as a woman in ministry means that you are able to verbalize how the Bible and your theology have made it possible for you to embrace your true self. That the biblical stories and the testimony you have heard from the pages of scripture have had a claim on your identity construction. That you know who you are not only because you know *whose* you are, but because you have allowed that identity to shape deeply how you live and move in the world.

As a result, you will feel your power and others will see it in you. You will then not live in a performative contradiction. Your identity, your authenticity, will be deeply connected to your vocation. Those to whom you minister will sense this coalescence of what you do and who you are; this, then, is true power because the power you have is grounded solely in the power of being who you are.

In many respects, the way in which the Bible is used to validate one's authentic self in ministry is also applicable to how the Bible can be used to validate women in ministry. As a woman in ministry, you need to know that these are related. The same biblical claims are being used to make similar yet different arguments.

Certainly, we could venture down the road of biblical claims that have been meaningful to many in terms of affirmation of call. Often, these biblical phrases that seem to support the importance of our unique selves in our call to ministry arise from the prophets. "I have called you by name; you are mine" from the prophet Isaiah (43:1); "Before I created you in the womb I knew you" (Jer 1:5). Moreover, these call stories are typically followed by excuses from the prophet of why he is not qualified for the task God has asked of him. Even Paul's call story fits this mold, particularly as it is narrated in Acts—the professional persecutor of Christians becomes apostle to the Gentiles.

Of course, this resonates deeply with our own need to be affirmed in our individual calls, that despite our failings and shortcomings, our inadequacies and lack of certain perceived necessary skills for ministry, God calls us anyway, limitations and all. It also touches the human need for redemption, forgiveness, and grace, which are all essential components of ministry and of life.

We are all very well aware that we are not flawless, that we enter ministry with a set of baggage all our own, that we would rather no one open up and look in. There are many in ministry whose sense of call and understanding of their call is deeply rooted in the prophetic call narratives. This is fine for some, but it does not have to be for all, and how it is interpreted is the critical issue. That is, the flaws and the failings can quickly dissolve into a badge of ministerial honor (the more flaws you have, the more miraculous your ministry will be), and those of us who look back on our rather average lives or who knew that ministry was our calling all along wonder where and how to fit in. This narrative has also resulted in a vast resource for excuses, for acceptance of mediocrity, and for a lack of striving for excellence. The church and its leaders have become the island of misfit ministers, which is just fine because God loves us just the way we are. But even in these stories of imperfect humans being called, we must acknowledge that God calls us to be more than who we were and to seek after a new identity in God.

The significance in all of this is to know yourself. Is the calling of the prophets really how you sense your call to ministry? If it is, embrace it and embrace it fully, but know fully and deeply how it is your story and how it reflects your own identity because of the extent to which some of these phrases and stories have become default settings for many.

A biblical imagination for authenticity in ministry, however, has to be your own. While the biblical imagination may be a narrative that confirms one's call and is meaningful for claiming power in the midst of imperfection, the starting point is less than advantageous for a woman in ministry. Again, the starting place matters deeply. To unlock the power of being a woman in ministry, authenticity has to start with who you are, rather than who you are not. Why? Because the narrative you use to describe your true self should not start from a place of negativity, of deficiency. It is true that in these stories God sees your true self, sees what you cannot see, and there is something extraordinarily powerful in that claim. At the same time, this does not have to translate into inherent worthlessness without God's salvific activity. Theologies that insist on the sheer depravity of humanity must eventually come to terms with how they articulate the meaning of being made in the image of God and God's decision for the incarnation.

We tend toward certain biblical summaries like that outlined above. "I am just like the prophets who resisted God's call, just like David, who made mistakes, and so therefore, I can be a part of God's ministry, too." While there is nothing theologically wrong with this claim, it has become a rather tired and worn-out suitcase that has taken this trip one too many times, particularly for women in ministry. When it comes to unlocking the power of women in ministry, are there other biblical briefs, other theological truths that express the importance of authenticity and truth of identity in ministry, ones that do not originate from a place of inherent deficit?

A biblical imagination for authenticity in ministry has to make the larger, more sweeping claim for the radical individuality of the people who end up in service to God and God's love for the world. The biblical rationale for authenticity, and why authenticity is essential for ministry, is God's commitment to radical diversity. Representation of the fullness of the incarnation is inherent to God's vision and version of church and ministry.

GENDER AND IDENTITY

One of the most persistent challenges for women when it comes to identity construction and discovering your authentic self is how much of that identity construction is connected to expectations specifically about the gender assigned to you at birth, whether or not it is authentic. The truth is also that you have different identities, intersecting identities, yet much of who you are is connected to your gender. The question you need to ask is to what extent your conceptualization of your identity is compartmentalized or integrated. The integration of identity as a woman is more challenging because so much of how we are identified is tied to cultural expectations, judgment, and competition based on our gender. KEY NUMBER TWO focused on expectations of women with regard to their bodies and their looks in particular. KEY NUMBER THREE will look at expectations of gender that are directly tied to gender as it determines societal roles in relation to leadership characteristics.

Self-talk is sometimes the only recourse you will have. What will be the narrative you will tell yourself? Negotiating all of these issues takes advanced planning. It is anticipating these issues ahead of time and deciding, before they surface, how you will respond and how you will choose to negotiate them. This strategy will also be true in the next chapter, on sexism. The fundamental means by which to deal with the inevitable and pervasive sexism in the church is to know it is coming. The same is true with issues of gender in the church. Although the church has made significant advances in its understanding and acceptance of nontraditional relationships and families and is beginning to work through the idea of nonbinary identities/expressions, for the most part, the church is still a very traditional institution, and most congregations operate within that traditionalism.

GENDER EXPECTATIONS FOR HOME AND FAMILY

The first set of expectations connected to gender arises out of relationship assumptions. If you are not married, the expectation is that you want to fall in love, get married, and have children, preferably with someone of the opposite sex. The congregation will want you to date and will likely "help" you do so with various and sundry matchmaking actions. One pastor shared, "I've had one homebound member of my current call try to set me up with her single, 58-year-old insurance man because 'Two single people should get together.'" Another added, "I was asked how I would handle dating in a small town where there weren't really any single people. I'm not sure if that's objectively sexist or not, but it came across as 'how're you going to find another husband without stealing someone else's?'" You will need to decide how you want to handle these attempts, and how you plan to respond to the inappropriate questions that will be asked. It is essential that you make it clear you will not date a person in the congregation. If you have people set you up and it does not end well, you will need to have already considered how you will negotiate that relationship.

Dating itself will be a challenge, should you choose to do so, because once again, the inappropriate questions will abound: "Is this person the one?" "Do you think you will get married?" "When will you get married?" Many people, particularly in congregations, lack a self-censor, regularly crossing social boundaries without notice and regard for how it affects you. Why particularly in congregations? There are several reasons. First, since they invite you into the most intimate moments of their lives, they think they should be a part of (or at least know about) yours. Secondly, and simultaneously, for the most part they really do care for you—they want to love you; they want to reciprocate the care you give to them. That makes handling these situations all the more difficult because you have the potential to hurt their feelings. Third, the unspoken truth is that they worry about how your relationship will affect them. That is, will you relocate? Will you spend more time with him or her and less time tending to their needs? Will it take time away from your church work? Will you leave the church to follow your partner's job? (This is still the expectation if you are a heterosexual woman and get married, that your career will take a backseat to that of your husband.) One pastor shared, "At the end of a very long train ride today to move from Philly to Raleigh with my two small kiddos, the train host volunteer asked: What's your husband do? Me: He's finishing his PhD. We're moving down here for my job. THV: Oh, and what do you do? Stay home with these two? Me: No, we're moving for my new job. I'm a priest at Christ Church in Raleigh. THV: You're a what now? Me: *sigh.*"

If you are married, it is likely that the gender expectation of women in ministry that will exert the most influence and be the most difficult to navigate is motherhood. If you are already a mother, there is a whole set of expectations when it comes to ministry. If you are not a mother, the expectation is that you want to be one, and it is just a question of when. There will be hopes for you in that direction, questions about your time frame for starting a family, most of which will be inappropriate and, if you are interviewing for a position in ministry, illegal. Most of the time, however, churches appear to assume that the law does not apply to ministry and they will ask questions about your relationships and your family plans. They will wonder, out loud or silently, if your spouse can take on the primary parental role to support your work at the church. If your spouse is of the same sex, this will incur another host of questions around expectations, realistic and not.

Here again, you will need to determine ahead of time how you want to respond to these questions, and you will also need to anticipate how you will feel about them. You need to think about how to react to questions about becoming a mother if you have decided that you do not want a family. If you do not want children, the likely reaction will be shock and disbelief. If you are trying to have children and are having fertility issues, these questions will hurt and hurt deeply. If the questions are unanticipated, you will react from that place of hurt or defensiveness; it is preferable to anticipate the pain and have a thoughtful, boundary-defining response ready.

If you become pregnant, anticipate another host of inquiries, which begin from the moment you find out. You need to decide when and how you will tell the congregation. If you miscarry, do you want them to accompany you in this grief or do you want it to remain personal? Most will be happy for your pregnancy, but others who are having fertility issues will be resentful and even angry. They will move to irrational theological explanations to make sense of their plight compared to your wish being granted—that because you are a pastor, a minister in the church, you are more religious, have more faith, and God will most certainly answer your prayers before theirs. Questions will arise—in a way that they would not for men in ministry who are starting a family—about how this will affect your work. In negotiating the terms of your position, if you plan to get pregnant or adopt, you need to set clear expectations for, and agreements about, parental leave. These cannot be assumed. The church is not any "nicer" than secular institutions to women, or their partners, who have just given birth—and, in fact, could be worse. You cannot assume that the leaves granted your friends in the secular world will be the same or better in the church.

Once the baby is born, there is another set of issues that surface, primarily how much the baby becomes a child of the whole congregation. They will want to hold it and touch it, and if you are a new mother, there is nothing more terrifying than having countless hands on your baby. This is all the more frightening if your child is born prematurely or with health issues that turn the common cold into a life-threatening illness. You will need to decide how to handle the desire of people to care for your baby, what boundaries you will erect, and how you will maintain them in the face of almost certain pushback. Will you allow your parishioners to visit you in your home? If so, how long will you invite them to stay? Will you set up a way for them to bring you food, whether or not that involves hosting them?

If you are a single mother, anticipate the misgivings as to how you can possibly serve a church and be a mother at the same time. Depending on the age of your child/children, will you do day care? Who will care for them when you need to be at church? What if there's an emergency at church? Will you bring them along? Do you have a backup plan? Will the church be shortchanged because your children come first?

If you are a clergy couple, all of the above will necessitate negotiation and renegotiation as your children grow. If both of you have Sunday morning responsibilities, are you comfortable with the church nursery? Do you want to determine designated baby holders? How will you handle breast-feeding if you have chosen to do so, or how will you handle the judgment if you do not? Will you nurse in between services? During services, if your responsibilities are over? How will you communicate your absence from worship to nurse? Or to pump? You will also need to determine how to handle the expectations that while the baby has two parents, you will still be thought of as the primary caregiver, even if you and your spouse have worked out a system of shared parenting. If your spouse is the primary caregiver (regardless of gender) and this is known by the congregation, how will you respond to questions that wonder how you can possibly be away from your children all day long? How will you handle the post-birth comments about your body, your weight, how you look, what you wear, your diet, or your plan to lose the baby weight? All of these are issues that will arise and need to be considered before the exhaustion of late pregnancy, the potential of postpartum depression, and early infancy takes their toll.

If you are partnered, what kind of role will your partner have? You have to set this out together on the front end and establish those expectations immediately. How will your partner handle the demands on your time, because the church, if allowed, will take it all? Even if your boundaries around family time are excellent, the church will try to take more time than you are willing to give. It is necessary to be deliberate about tending to the intimate relationships that will sustain us through the ups and downs of ministry.

If you are married and have children, the church is both wonderful and challenging. It is wonderful because your schedule is flexible. You can often determine your workweek and adapt it to the demands of your children and your family life. It is challenging because the congregation will have expectations of your children quite unlike the expectations they have for any other children in the congregation. How they behave in church, what they wear to church, and how often they come to church will be closely examined and often criticized—as will you. One pastor shared, "I was told my child wasn't welcome at any church event or in worship because then 'people will see you as a mother instead of a minister.'" If your children are older, and especially if this is a second or third career for you, it may be helpful to have a conversation with them about these unrealistic expectations and how to handle them. What will you expect of your own children? Do they have to go to every youth event or on every trip? How will you navigate church responsibilities and other demands for their time, such as friends, sports, and school activities? Anyone who has been a "preacher's kid" knows very well these expectations.

Regardless of how far women have come with regard to home responsibilities and shared parenting, the expectation remains that the traditional understandings of wife and mother still apply to you, and that you are the one who has primary parenting and domestic responsibility. You will inevitably have questions or comments with regard to the care of your children and how you "balance" everything, making sure everything is running smoothly both at church and at home. People will volunteer to help you so that you can go home and take care of your family. While an offer seems generous on the surface, it is often a passive-aggressive lose-lose scenario. If you decline the help, you are a bad parent, but if you accept, then you aren't really committed to the church.

GENDER EXPECTATIONS OF LEADERSHIP CHARACTERISTICS

The moment we begin to fear the opinions of others & hesitate to tell the truth that is in us . . . the floods of light and life no longer flow into our souls.

—*Elizabeth Cady Stanton*

Before we address leadership characteristics connected to gender, we need to acknowledge the general surprise and resistance you will experience as a woman in ministry, particularly if you are clergy. Others will consistently question your leadership, especially if you serve with a male colleague. One pastor wrote, "We recently added a new evening service. My male colleague and I co-officiated the entire thing, including communion. Afterward, a man comes up to me, points at my male colleague a few feet away, and says, 'So is that the minister?'" Another lamented, "I had a community member come up to me in a public place and say, 'I went to your x-y-z service the other night. It was really good...for a woman.'" Another pastor shared that when she was called to her church, an elderly gentleman said he'd leave. He'd had a bad experience with a woman pastor. Someone asked him if he'd ever had a bad experience with a male pastor. He said he had. So would he leave if they called a male? "Hmm. No, I'd never thought of it that way..." The image, still, that comes to mind for most people when they think of a pastor is male. Try a Google image search for "pastor" and then see how long it takes to find a picture of a female pastor.

Another set of expectations for women in ministry directly tied to gender has to do with particular leadership characteristics associated specifically with women. These are usually connected with motherhood or being motherly in some way. Leadership characteristics valued in women are those that represent nurturing, empowering, supporting, and caretaking. The problem arises, of course, when a woman in a leadership role does not exhibit these expected leadership traits. There is an automatic disconnect when these anticipated features of women in leadership are not manifested in a woman in leadership.

There will be a host of gender expectations around women in ministry with regard to gender roles in the church. Will you start a women's Bible study or do women's ministry and retreats? You will be the one asked to make coffee for meetings with both clergy and laity, and to provide food and beverages, if the parish assistant is unavailable. One pastor shared, "I am routinely asked for my input on stupid details regarding meals/luncheons (I'm really curious if this happens to my male counterparts, but I have a feeling they're not asked about napkin color or punch preferences as often as I am)." Another wrote that there is the "constant expectation that I be both pastor and 'pastor's wife'...I am always asked to bake pies and cookies for church events." You will be the one assumed as host. You will likely be expected to take on "secretarial" duties if needed in meetings.

If a woman does not exhibit these characteristics, then her ability to lead is immediately called into question. What kind of leader is she if she does not demonstrate the expected characteristics of a *woman* in leadership? This means that often the resistance to your leadership has less to do with you and more to do with the fact that you are not representing the leadership traits a person believes should be inherent in women who are in leadership roles. Like many things with regard to being a woman in ministry, the issue, then, is not the issue.

Furthermore, rather than being respected for manifesting leadership characteristics that are valued in men, women are disavowed and misinterpreted. That is, the same leadership trait expected of and respected in men will, at best, be interpreted differently and at its worst, lead to defamation and degradation with derogatory claims about the woman who seems to embody them. We know these labels well: bitch, pushy, stubborn. "A man who doesn't help is 'busy'; a woman is 'selfish.'"[2] The pairings usually go something like this: the boss/bossy; persuasive/pushy; dedicated/selfish; neat/vain; smooth/show-off.[3] Leadership traits and values are segregated by gender, and to excel in areas outside of your prescribed role is to invite suspicion and discomfort. Associated with this list of double-standard leadership traits is vocabulary women seem to use more than men, which is then assumed to undermine their communication and their leadership.[4] These include the terms "just"[5] and "sorry."[6] At the same time, the obsession with how women talk is precisely the point.[7] The recommendations for our speech are as much a control of women as they are meant to make us sound more like men.

Furthermore, other assumptions about your leadership abilities and style will be assessed based on assumed gender or what is culturally considered to make someone female. A number of pastors shared that their moods were attributed to menstruation and menopause. That which is considered to be inherent to being female is then blamed for irritability or instability.[8]

An unfortunate result of these kinds of opinions of and reactions to your ministry is self-doubt. Over time, and often sooner rather than later, as others question your leadership potential, so will you. This can lead to another period of time in your call to ministry when you have to navigate the imposter syndrome: you thought you were a good leader, people affirmed these traits in you, and others told you that you were a natural leader. All of a sudden, you see this affirmation unravel, so much so that you begin to convince yourself that the dissenting voices are the ones speaking the truth, rather than the ones that remind you to be true to yourself.

THE MYTH OF BALANCE

Balance is a myth. It is simply not possible to keep even the important things in your life in perfect balance every day, all the time. At the same time, this is a rather ubiquitous mantra in ministry and in life. Maintaining balance has become another mark of achievement: "Look how well she balances work and home!" It can also become that perceived attainable achievement that is to your detriment and your downfall if you think it is realistic or within your reach.

Some actual reflection on what is assumed in the concept of balance makes its attainability all the more absurd. To imagine that all of your responsibilities—your multiple roles and your own self—can be at equal weight all the time is simply not reasonable. Circumstances will demand that various aspects of who you are and what you do in your life receive more attention at times.

The myth of balance also can be debilitating when we think that it is entirely in our control. Circumstances arise that tip the scale regardless of how much effort you put into keeping the weight even. If the weight is off-kilter, the question becomes how you respond to that instability. When an unreasonable amount of effort is directed toward preserving equilibrium, there is less energy to direct toward strategies for dealing with what happens when the symmetry is upset.

In the end, the myth of balance can also be a rather hazardous affair. When its root image is that of the equal spread of weight to avoid falling, or staying in one position so that you do not fall, the result of a lack of balance is falling, and falling hard. No one wants to fall, not only because it hurts, but also because it is often a public event. Witnessed by others, it reveals something about you that is "off" whether that be physical or metaphorical. We right ourselves after that embarrassing fall, not having learned the lesson of inevitable disaster, determined to do better with keeping all things equal.

Of course, the attractiveness of balance is rooted in the idea of making sure that all that is important in your life receives equal attention. This goal should not be an ideal but an essential to how you live your life. At the same time, the important aspects of your life cannot always receive equal amounts of attention. Yet, knowing what is important in your life can be a critical point of entry when it comes to a discussion about balance; it is certainly a better entry point than any abstract aspirations of what balance should be. That is, being able to identify those aspects of your life that are not only important to you, but also the ones that make up who you are, is the first step toward a full life, a life that is authentic to who you are and not out of reach of who you know yourself to be— although this might not necessarily be a balanced life. Generalities about the benefits of securing balance will not mean much, and, as noted above, might even have negative effects unless these general claims are lodged in concrete life commitments. As a result, the attention you give to determining those essential aspects of your life that make up your identity is attention better directed than that which aims toward theoretical views of a balanced life.

Crucial to unlocking your power as a woman in ministry is to know and keep tabs on those things in your life that have been vital to your identity construction, that ground you in your authenticity, and that would be devastating to your sense of self were they not there. It is tiring to be yourself, which is why constant connection to your core commitments will make a sense of balance possible. It is very important to identify your core commitments that make up who you are and realize the truth that all of these are in play, all of the time. There is no one core commitment that is more important than the other. Here again, however, beware of the myth of balance: even the core commitments cannot all bear equal weight all of the time. There is no magic number for these commitments, nor should the number necessarily be the same for each person. Typically, these core commitments coalesce around work and vocation, family, friends, and personal interests. This act of identifying these core commitments has to be deeply personal: what is important to you and only you and crucial to your authenticity as a person and as a person in ministry.

What does any of this have to do with your power as a woman in ministry? Power is perceived individually and relationally when it appears that you "have it all together." Translated, having it all together refers to what was discussed earlier: that you have a solid sense of your commitments and what is important to you, and you are able to prioritize those commitments even in the midst of changing dynamics and demands, both in situations and with your time. Of course, there may be some people who do not like you, not because they do not like you personally, but because they are threatened by someone who has her stuff together and who lives out of her truth. Genuine power, however, when it comes to a balanced life, means that you are able to be truthful about these shifting realities when it comes to allegiances. Effective power means that you are truthful about when your life is "out of balance" and that you take action toward realignment before it all comes crashing down around you.

In practical terms, this approach to "maintaining balance" requires constant renegotiation, sometimes daily. That is, you assess regularly and frequently where, how, and why your commitments have come into a state of imbalance. If one commitment in your life is receiving or has received the most attention for a while (likely for good reasons), how can you bring some of the others into focus, and which ones need more focus than others? For some, this strategy of realignment and recalibration may seem exhausting. Yet, more exhausting is the energy it takes to maintain a myth.

Chapter Three

BALANCE AND BOUNDARIES

Let me listen to me and not to them.

—*Gertrude Stein*

Attention to the role of balance in your ministry will succeed in upholding your life and personal commitments that represent your identity. These commitments are then embodied in ministry so that your ministry is authentically you. Balance takes extraordinary intentionality. At the same time, paying attention to balance and reflecting on it is also critical because it is the place to start when it comes to boundaries. You need to protect yourself and you have a right to protect yourself. Keeping clear, healthy boundaries will be difficult, if not impossible, if the work on identity and authenticity as they are manifested in balance and core commitments has not been done. If you do not have a good sense of what is essential to you and what commitments identify who you are, the levels of boundary crossing will be many and dangerous.

The church excels at crossing personal boundaries. It succeeds like no other entity in your life in usurping your time, energy, commitments, and even your spirit. Why? There is an unspoken theological reason for these demands on who you are—self-sacrifice. Just as Jesus sacrificed all, just as the disciples sacrificed their lives, ministers in the church are expected to engage in that same kind of self-sacrificial behavior. Yet this expectation of self-sacrifice can quickly lead to a giving up of yourself and giving up on yourself, who you truly are. We all know that the church will take all of who you are, all the time, if these boundaries are not set. For women in ministry, this reality is exponentially increased because we feel an obligation to give more time and to give more of ourselves, so as to prove to others that we are worthy of this call because self-sacrifice is seen as a maternal, feminine value. The default tendency will be to over-function: to do everything ourselves, to take on too much of the work. But your worthiness of this call has to come from your own identity, your own person, your own sense of authenticity and truth. It cannot be based or dependent on the work of ministry.

What are these boundary crossings that occur in ministry? In chapter 4, we will discuss boundary issues specifically related to sexuality. The boundaries that need attention here in this chapter are those crossings that can be more difficult to deflect and deter. They include time, skill set for ministry, and identity/authenticity.

First, the boundary of your time is easily and regularly crossed by the demands of ministry. In general, the perception of ministry and its tasks is befuddlement at what we actually do. This is especially true for the task of preaching. If you are part of the preaching staff at your church, anticipate that people simply have no idea how much it takes to prepare a sermon. Most would be absolutely shocked to learn that it can take up to twenty hours. Nor do they understand that, really, you are never *not* working on your sermon, because the entirety of your week is going about ministry with the text in mind for proclamation. You have to protect the process and therefore you have to protect your time.

The church will always want more of your time. One of the challenges of ministry, of course, is that the "job" is never over, never done. Yes, like other jobs, there will always be more to do. But unlike other jobs, what needs to be done frequently has something to do with the very soul of a person. While this may be an overstatement, it will not feel like an overstatement when you are doing ministry. The boundary crossing of your time also means that the church will feel free not only to take as much of your time as possible, but to take it from any given part of your day or week—evenings, days off, it is all fair game. While there are many benefits and blessings to being the manager of your own time, the downside is that the church can, and will, ask for your time 24/7. The visit that you planned for tomorrow now needs to happen today. The call that comes in the middle of the night. The surgery that goes longer than anticipated. The work can quickly take up the entirety of your day. Two helpful strategies by which to handle these time demands are a return to your core commitments and the twenty-one-blocks-per-week time management strategy.

Your time will remain your own when you are clear with yourself and others about your core commitments. If these core commitments do not receive the time they deserve, you will feel that loss, you will sense imbalance, or, if one or more of your core commitments are people, they will feel it. They will either express it (and here is where the honesty of children is essential) and you should give them permission to call you on it, or they will keep it to themselves, causing relational strain. You need to have others tell you when they are not getting the time they need from you. When you do not honor your time, it is not just your time that is at stake, but the time for which others count on you. Not only are you letting them down, you are putting the relationship in peril. If your boundary of time is crossed, then it also crosses the time boundary of others.

The second strategy for negotiating time and boundaries is to think about your week as made up of twenty-one blocks, three blocks per day, not including time for sleep or meals. Your "work" day should consist of two of those three blocks, with a space between for lunch. For example, if you know you will be doing visits all afternoon and be at church in the evening, the morning should be "off" time or your time. For this to work, however, you have to invoke an aspect of ministry that can be your best friend when it comes to protecting your time—confidentiality. We know that confidentiality is essential, and is even mandated for ministry to protect the personal time and issues of the people you serve. At the same time, confidentiality can also mean that you do not have to disclose your whereabouts to anyone. You would never divulge to your administrative assistant that one of your afternoon visits was visiting someone in the psychiatric unit of a hospital. You are simply out visiting. If you feel compelled to explain why you will not arrive at the church office right at 9:00 a.m. on the dot, but rather after lunch before you go out on visits, your explanation can be as simple as "I have an off-site appointment/ meeting." And you do. With yourself. You owe no one a justification of your self-care. If you offer the real reason for your morning absence, your time immediately becomes an object of scrutiny. "You only work on Sundays, right?" is an assumption of ministers in the church that is alive and well. The perception of ministry and its tasks is wonderment at what we actually do.

Second, the boundaries of your ministry skill set will regularly be crossed. That is, while you may have been clear about the gifts for ministry that you bring, while you may have offered a detailed list of your particular experiences and interests, the reality is that most churches want, although they are not open about it, a Jane-of-all-trades. Of course, this is a lot of what ministry is. At the same time, if you accept tasks or responsibilities that move out of your particular strengths for ministry, this time will be taken away from the areas of ministry that you have honed, that you enjoy, and that potentially arise from your passions. Learning new skills can be a positive challenge, but it can also draw attention away from what gives you joy. If you are consistently asked to move into areas of ministry in which you have little training or to which you have had little exposure, you become fair at a lot, but lack excellence in few, thus diminishing your effectiveness, even your power. In some instances, it may very well be a technique by which actively to weaken your power.

There will also be ministry areas that are assumed to be your gifts because of your gender. For example, as a woman, others will anticipate that you must be very good at pastoral care and that it is probably your major strength in ministry, even if neither is true. You will need to determine why you are being asked to add another responsibility to your ministry, whether it is truly within your skill set, and whether you are being asked to take it on simply because of your gender. What are you required to do that your male colleagues are not? You will need to decide what you feel comfortable in saying yes to, and what you do not. Furthermore, if there is a ministry area that needs attention, the likelihood is that you will be approached before your male colleagues with the assumption that, in general, women are more agreeable than men and will acquiesce to perceived need more often than men. The truth is, men are applauded for setting good boundaries and women are not. Honesty with yourself around what you can and cannot do, in assessing what your gifts really are, is essential for maintaining boundaries.

The boundary crossings that occur with respect to your identity and your authenticity are the most difficult to avert. These are the moments when your core commitments are at risk, when the very truth of who you are is taken advantage of or abused. In this case, the characteristics, traits, and things that you have determined are important to you, that make up the core of your being, are manipulated for the gain of the church, particularly the church as institution and the church as system. These are the circumstances in which the things you are asked to do, or the things that are taken away from you, will directly affect who you are at your core. These are the situations in which you feel, deep down, that you are being discounted, that you are being used—that your identity is not in the equation at all, but only what you can do for the other. The risk here is to give in when these situations arise, not to stand up for who you are or call out the injustice. And all too often, this is exactly what happens with women in leadership, particularly in ministry. Trust, especially when it comes to your sense of self, has to be earned. It cannot be assumed.

This may sound pessimistic, even cynical and lacking hope for the church. Yet, the hope that the church is different is at the very heart of the issue: the hope that the church will not be like other institutions that try to run you over for their own gain; that the church holds sacred each and every person called by God. Sadly, this is not true. The hope lies not in the church as it currently exists, but in our own power to make it be the church—a place set apart from the world. A space that is truly holy. The church, like all systems, like all people, succumbs to the kind of power that corrupts, that usurps, that maintains the bottom line, and certainly does not respect the well-being of those who feel called to its service.

Preserving the boundary around your identity and your authenticity means learning how to say no. Saying no is extraordinarily difficult. We do not want to disappoint or displease; this is human nature. It is human nature to please and to be liked, and saying no certainly runs the risk of leading to disapproval. This is especially true for women, who have more of a desire to please and who have been socialized to have a desire to please, in part because it has been necessary in order to advance professionally and vocationally. At the same time, no explanation is necessary when you say no, despite how your no will be treated. When a man declines a request on the basis of his principles, this is construed as admirable and honorable. When a woman does the same, she is disagreeable. Critical in all of this is to make sure that what makes you who you are is not overrun, overshadowed, or, worse, extinguished in your call to ministry. You are living your truth when you are not over-adapting. Your light will shine brightly when you are true to yourself. But it is also true that others, even in the church, will try to extinguish your light. How do you know when your light is going out? When you feel like your soul, the essence of who you are, is almost unraveling, crumbling; when you sense that you cannot tap into your creativity and your passion. Boundary maintenance is, in part, protecting your light while also letting your light shine, for the sake of yourself and for the sake of others who need to see it.

One way that this issue gets articulated with regard to boundaries is the question of self-care. You have to take responsibility for your own self-care, which is why it is deemed "self" care—no one else will do it for you. Why is self-care so essential for ministry? Because it is when you get tired that there is the possibility to let people extinguish your light. Self-care is soul care, heart things. It is nourishing your soul. But self-care is not always deemed a positive trait in ministry. While this is certainly a defensible description for keeping that which is important to you close and tending those things that keep your soul healthy and whole, there will be resistance to this in ministry if this kind of language is used regularly.

While people in the church are all for self-care, for some reason they think that persons who work in the church are not in need of it. The "for some reason" is actually rooted in certain expected characteristics of ministers: selflessness, a radical orientation to the other, and the sense of doing God's work, which never ends. You can talk about self-care as much as you want, but it will fall on ears that will question it, even resist it, especially when it comes to women ministers in the church. Why? Because society perpetuates the belief that inherent to women is self-sacrifice. Women in ministry are not in need of self-care because they willingly and regularly give of themselves. When it comes to unlocking your power as a woman in ministry, being able to articulate your core commitments with certitude and strength is essential.

FINDING YOUR VOICE—AND KEEPING IT

It is not "good" voices or "bad" voices that I am listening for, but voices that come from somewhere near the heart and that do not seem afraid to be heard.

—*Barbara Brown Taylor*

Another category by which to construe authenticity is that of voice. Voice is more than simply speaking; it engages the whole self—mind, body, spirit, your true self. Using another category, such as this one, helps us access elements of identity and authenticity in a different way and can become another set of practical strategies for going about living into your own sense of truth. How we understand voice can be lodged in four categories: theological, personal, practical, and communal.

Voice is a theological concept because utterance is directly connected to how God expresses God's own self. God spoke, and in doing so God revealed God's self. Speech is revelation. Voice is intimately tied to theological revelation. In ministry, our speaking is not just our own but for the sake of God's own expression. We speak, in part, for God, or God speaks through us. God counts on us to emit the words of God and the Word of God so that others might hear the promises of God in their own lives. Moreover, your voice and God's voice intersect in your expression. God's Word and words are interpreted in your utterance. For example, when you read scripture aloud, that act alone is an act of interpretation. The words you emphasize—your tone, timbre, pitch, vocal variety, volume, and expressions—all communicate meaning. In that reading, you are communicating what is important to you about that scripture passage. You are communicating what matters to you, at least for this time, place, and purpose. You are communicating, in part, who you are theologically because of what you have chosen to emphasize and what you have decided to give less import.

As a result, voice is very personal. What you have to say, how you say it, your vocabulary, your accent, your intonation, when you speak up and when you don't reveal your identity and your character. Your voice gives oral expression to what is deep in your soul, what is important to you. To believe in your own voice, you have to believe in your identity and your own experience and believe that it deserves to be spoken out loud, it needs to be heard, and it needs to be heard by others. Believing in your voice means remembering who you are, which sometimes will demand an intentional reclaiming of your identity.

To have a sense of how personal voice really is, think about when, how, and by whom your voice may have been silenced. What were the circumstances? What was the situation? What were you prevented from saying? How did you feel? When you are not allowed to speak, when you are shut up, it feels as if your light has been extinguished.

When you realize how personal voice is, it shapes significantly how you do ministry. For example, it shapes how you interpret scripture. When you know what it feels like to be silenced, then you notice those who have been silenced in the biblical texts. You notice who gets to talk and who doesn't. You take an interpretive stance that is committed to allowing the silenced to be heard. You give voice to those who so desperately wish to speak.

Your voice also shapes how you do pastoral care. Who in your congregation do you sense wants to speak, but has never been invited to or has never been allowed to speak? Who has something to contribute, but has not figured out how to let others know? How can you help them articulate their theology, opinions, and faith? Because of who you are, a woman in ministry, a woman in leadership in the church, you will have other women—and even men—who will come to you to help them find their voice. When you are able to utter your truth, you automatically invite others to imagine the same. You invite them to envisage that this is possible for them. But they will need your help. You will need to accompany them to give voice to who they are.

We can think about voice and identity from a very practical perspective. Your voice is, quite literally, your voice—how you express yourself verbally. This becomes a critical point for women in ministry because of the physical nature of women's voices. Women's voices tend to be higher pitched and harder to hear. It will be essential to assess the nature of your voice and whether or not it reflects the power of your own person. You will undoubtedly receive comments on your voice that, while critical of its timbre or pitch, more often than not originate from a resistance to what it means to listen to a woman's expression of God's word. The concern is located less in the person's hearing challenges and more in the person's inability to hear the ways in which a woman's voice is now another source of hearing God speak.

The practical issues around voice are crucial, and reflecting on the concrete components of voice must begin with a general knowledge about the essentials of public speaking. As a leader, you are a public figure. You will be called to speak in public on a regular basis in situations that include, but are not limited to, preaching. In these moments, you are communicating your power as a woman in ministry. If your general presence as a communicator, which includes your voice and your image, is not given attention, it makes it far more difficult to communicate your power and to convince people of your power in other ministry settings. Furthermore, your power will be acknowledged if there is a strong correlation between who you are as a public figure in public settings and how you present yourself in more private and individual moments of ministry.

While we should be able to assume that a fear of public speaking is less for those who answer a call to ministry, it nevertheless still brings with it its challenges separate from the fear. These challenges coalesce around identifiable yet false perceptions that surface in public speaking and that need to be named because these misguided assumptions can lead to the questioning of one's ability to carry out the call to ministry. The first perception that the act of public speaking exposes is the sense of needing to be perfect; yet, we must realize that perfection is not possible. The second needed change in perception is the move from "I can't tolerate any anxiety or discomfort when I am speaking in front of people" to "I can stand discomfort and it will pass." One significant issue with regard to this second perception is for you to know how your body exhibits discomfort and stress. For example, unintentional gestures, sweaty palms, and dry mouth are all physical manifestations of anxiety. You need to know what your body does, and practice countermeasures to deter their potential effect on your presentation. A third perception is the unrealistic claim that a negative review is the end the world. Although unfortunate and uncomfortable, you will survive a negative review. A fourth perception says, "If I fail, then I am a failure." The reality, of course, is that failure at one task does not make you a failure in others. The fifth and final untrue perception that arises in public speaking connects a poor evaluation or rating with worthlessness. Yet, even if you are given a poor evaluation, that does not mean that you have to lose your self-esteem or your confidence.

It is important to notice that each of these misguided perceptions directly connects to one's identity, one's core being. This is because public speaking is an extraordinary act of vulnerability. Ministry involves being a public leader, a public voice, called upon to share in multiple public settings the truth of faith and how that truth is embodied in you. Moments of public speaking are unquestionably moments of power, both owned and perceived. These moments must be managed for the power they have, the power that you can claim in them, and the power that then can carry over into your ministry.

Basic public speaking effectiveness is centered in five areas: volume, fluency, vocal variety, clarity, and physical image. Tending these five essential aspects of public speaking is necessary because how you speak is directly connected to your credibility and believability.

To live into your power as a woman in ministry necessitates that you are fully aware of the dimensions of public speaking and what difference each makes for your effectiveness as a public figure. The first element essential to effectiveness in a public role is volume. In fact, volume is always number one in importance. If your audience, your congregation, cannot hear you, they cannot be affected by what you say. Volume is also an indicator of confidence. Volume is directly connected to whether or not the audience perceives the speaker to be confident in her material. Volume is potentially the most important aspect of your voice to address and will certainly have the most impact on how you are perceived. In general, we do not speak loudly enough, although many of the people with whom we do ministry are hard of hearing. Your ability to speak loudly and clearly, especially in acoustically challenged places, will go a long way in your effectiveness as a woman in ministry. The truth is, most people expect women to talk softly. They also expect that they will have difficulty hearing you. Counteracting these expectations ahead of time will go a long way in allowing your voice to be heard.

There are three primary reasons why we do not speak loudly enough. The first is a lack of self-confidence. If we lack confidence in ourselves and in what we have to say, the solution tends to be to lower our volume. The second reason why we do not speak loudly enough is that we are generally not accustomed to the space. We are not used to having our voice fill a room, to reverberate around us, and initially this can be uncomfortable. You have to be prepared to fill a space no matter what the size and even without a PA system. The third reason why we do not speak loudly enough is that there is a socially acceptable volume, not always the same for men and women, which is the volume that is comfortable for both parties when talking one-on-one directly to another person. If you speak louder than that anticipated volume, you are labeled a "loud talker."

The second essential skill in public speaking is fluency, or the ability to speak without unintended pauses or breaks. While you may insert planned pauses and breaks in a speaking presentation (a very effective and even necessary tool), the unplanned pauses are detrimental to your effectiveness and your ability to be heard. Unplanned pauses or breaks are usually due to a lack of memory, knowledge, or adequate rehearsal. The best way to gain fluency is practice. While planned pauses have the potential to effect meaning and to allow your hearers to process something that has been said, unplanned pauses break the flow, impulse, and direction of a public presentation. Moreover, unplanned pauses tend to proliferate with "filler words" such as "umm," "uh," "just," "you know," "like," and so on. Filler words are distracting and have the negative potential of others' questioning your subject matter and mastery of it. Fluency is also directly connected to making successful eye contact while speaking publicly. The more fluent and comfortable you are with your sermon or presentation, the more you will be able to talk to people, rather than to your paper. The ability to connect with your listeners via eye contact communicates confidence in your message. It also succeeds in making a connection with your listeners, thus demonstrating vulnerability and intimacy. People will be more willing to listen to what you have to say and you will show how power works in moments of relationship, openness, and trust.

The third essential element for effectiveness in public speaking is vocal variety in volume, pace, pitch, tone, resonance, and timbre. Our human sensory apparatus is directed to novelty and contrast, so vocal variety becomes a critical component to effective communication. The extremes of vocal variety are the lack thereof (flat monotone) and random variation only for the sake of variety. Neither of those will be effective. Vocal variety should be that which we recognize as interpretive and providing meaning. The way you say it conveys as much meaning as what you say. The potential for vocal variety to legitimize and validate your speech cannot be overstated, yet the breadth of our capacity for vocal variety is generally vastly underutilized. This also demands much preparation time, both to determine your emphases and to practice them out loud.

The fourth element necessary for effectual speech is clarity. Clarity refers to two important features of public speaking: organizational clarity and vocal clarity. Clarity is rather simple: if your listeners cannot understand you, that is a problem. You need not just be clear but crystal clear, so that which you are trying to communicate can have the intended effect. Clarity has everything to do with the 65% / 40% / 10% rule in public speaking. While you are speaking, on average, the listeners only hear, process, and understand 65% of your presentation. After an hour, only 40% of your presentation is remembered. After three days, listeners can only recall 10% of your material. Given the subject matter related to ministry, we need to be diligent in our work toward increasing these percentages. If you want the faith lives of people to be affected by your words, your words have to be heard. This is even truer as a woman in ministry. You will need to develop these skills more than your male colleagues because people are more accustomed to listening to men in positions of leadership in the church.

Organizational clarity refers to the basic form and format of your presentation. For preaching, this is sermon design or the form of your sermon. For any kind of public presentation, the outline or structure is critical. You need to have a point, support for that point, and a direction of where you are going. Sequencing your sermon or speech is essential for clarity. This also means having clear directions or transitions in your sermon or presentation by which your listeners can follow where you are going, similar to using turn signals in a vehicle. All of this is for the sake of your message being heard. Fred Craddock notes, "It is a tragic error to assume that the Truth is its own evangelist...And those of us concerned to communicate the Christian gospel...must all the while follow the operational principle, *if it has been heard*. To effect that hearing is no small task."[9] Clarity also is brought about by the notes that you bring with you into the pulpit, the lectern, or in a binder or Bible, if you are not using a podium of any kind. For preaching, this is your sermon manuscript. Regardless of the genre, you need to imagine this as your "performance manuscript." That is, just like a musician would never bring a clean score to a performance, a public speaker would never have notes that do not represent attention to and instruction in delivery. Use indentation, paragraphing, bold, italics, handwritten notes—that is, use any and all devices to help you move through your presentation with clarity. This performance manuscript recognizes that what you have to say is not only the words on the page but how they sound. You are not finished with your sermon, or with any public presentation, until you have printed it out and practiced it out loud, making notes as to how you want to speak the words and how you want them to be heard.

It is in this practicing out loud that you are able to tend to vocal clarity. Vocal clarity includes articulation and enunciation. This aspect of public speaking is important not only for preaching and public speaking events, but also for one-on-one conversations. Most people have a propensity to mumble, to underuse their mouth, tongue, lips, jaw, and face in the execution of speech. Vocal clarity in public circumstances secures that your individual words will be heard and not lost in the space. This means, of course, emphasis on consonants, being careful not to drop or elide them. Vocal variety in dialogue is essential because persons who are hard of hearing read lips, and those persons who have difficulties hearing are no longer only the elderly in our congregations. More and more younger people are diagnosed with hearing loss, which means that as a leader in the church, you need to be vigilant about vocal articulation. Moreover, persons with hearing loss may not divulge their situation, either because they are embarrassed or because they do not want to call attention to themselves. Practicing articulation and enunciation may be uncomfortable at first and feel exaggerated, even silly. Yet you need to be able both to hear and to feel words so that they can be heard. Congregation members will be incredibly grateful for this simple act in your ministry—speaking clearly. They will be able to hear you, which you want and which they want, desperately, and they will sense that you care, that you realize these challenges and have taken the time to address them in your ministry. This attention to vocal clarity is an act toward unlocking your power as a woman in ministry. People will appreciate and acknowledge your strength in vocal expression that communicates power and confidence.

The fifth essential practical element toward success in public speaking is attention to physical image or presentation. Before you utter one word, your listeners have already determined whether or not they are interested in what you have to say by observing your behavior, your body language, and your appearance. How you present yourself correlates to how you will be heard—or not. First impressions are made within 7–15 seconds, and it is much more difficult to correct a negative first impression than it is to create a positive first impression. Even outside of public speaking, first impressions and how you present yourself are crucial as a person in ministry. While this may seem a most exhausting and even daunting reality, attention to presentation has a lasting effect on how your power is perceived. For a woman in ministry, how you present yourself is a high-stakes issue. KEY NUMBER TWO included discussion that needs to be brought to the forefront regarding attire for physical presentation. Your attire is the object of scrutiny and will be assessed, inasmuch as it reflects if and how you will be heard. When it comes to public presentations, you will have to choose carefully what to wear to ensure that your attire matches the moment and does not work against your presentation. Do women in ministry have to think about this more than their male colleagues in ministry? The answer to that question is an unequivocal "yes." Is it fair? No, it is not fair—it is simply the truth. How you use this truth, however, will have an impact on the efficacy of your power. If you choose to ignore this reality and not give attention to decisions about what to wear, particularly when in public settings, your power and perceptions of your power will be diminished. This means choosing outfits authentic to who you are that also fit the occasion.

Physical presentation is also about how you stand, whether that is behind a pulpit or lectern or out in front, and it is critical to public speaking. Standing tall with shoulders back intimates confidence and power but also vulnerability at the same time. Not standing up to your full height or hunching your shoulders will communicate the opposite. In public speaking, the audience assesses the stance of the speaker and decides immediately how the speech will go. This is called the mirror principle. The audience mirrors the confidence in you that they perceive you have in yourself. The power of your words begins with the power of your silence.

Also significant to your physical presentation is your use of gestures while you speak. Gestures communicate meaning as much as your words do, but they can also counter intended meaning if you are oblivious to how you naturally communicate with your body. For most, gestures are awkward at first and they feel forced. Yet, a well-placed gesture in a sermon or speech not only adds to the meaning of what is being said but also communicates that you are comfortable with your body. Even the mere awareness of gestures will prevent the nervous or unplanned ones. Just as anxiety manifests itself in physiological ways, it is also expressed in uncontrolled gestures. Like filler words, there are also filler gestures, in part because we are often completely unaware of our bodily movements. Yet gestures such as putting your hair behind your ear, pushing up your glasses, or playing with your ring are not only distracting and off-putting but pull people away from your message.

There are three strategies by which to address the practical issues of voice addressed above when it comes to unlocking your power as a woman in ministry. The first strategy is to review each of the elements listed above carefully and thoughtfully, with the result being an honest self-assessment. What could improve? What will you do to make those improvements happen? The second strategy is to enlist an outside evaluator—a friend, someone you trust from your congregation—to listen for each of these elements in your speaking and to give you truthful, regular feedback. The third strategy is to consider working with a professional vocal coach to maximize your communication skills. These practical issues when it comes to voice have the potential to take a lot of time and work, yet they are critical to your voice being heard. While we might resent such efforts, remembering our accountability to effect the hearing of the gospel puts such demands in perspective.

Voice is communal because it is fundamentally about communication for the sake of relationship. Finding, nurturing, and keeping your voice is a communal and corporate exercise. How your voice resonates and re-verberates in community is different from how it sounds individually. Just as the voice can bind many people into one community, it can take many people, in community, to nurture your voice; an important aspect of voice in ministry is to determine those persons and those places that can help you find, nurture, and keep your voice. Furthermore, you need to know you can trust your voice as much in how it resounds in community as in how it sounds individually. If you trust and like your voice only when you are alone, your voice has the possibility of not being heard. Hearing your voice in community takes some getting used to and takes some practice. At first, your voice voiced in community might sound different—is that really me? You might be surprised at what you can or cannot say in com-munity. You may wonder if what you say to yourself you should say to others. But this is when we have to remember that questions of voice are fundamentally theological. God voiced the world into existence because God chose to be in relationship. The Word became flesh because God knew that an individual voice gains power and meaning in relationship. God asks us to give voice to God's mercy because God's own voice can-not do it on its own. When you find your voice and give it utterance, you enter into God's communal voicing of love and forgiveness, grace and belonging.

CLOSING THOUGHTS

If you only trust people who do things that please you, there is no one you can trust. If you trust everyone, you are a fool. If you trust too soon, you are probably afraid of being rejected. If you trust too superficially, you may be easily betrayed. If you trust too late, you may never know what love is.

—*David Viscott, MD*

Identity/authenticity is finally about trust. It's about trusting in yourself, who you are and who you want to be. It's about believing that you can locate your trust in the person God has called you to be. This is not a blind trust that chooses to ignore when, how, and where your own sense of self trumps the worth of another. It's a trust that knows what it feels like to embody self-worth, and what inspires you the most is how you can make that true for others.

EXERCISES AND QUESTIONS FOR REFLECTION

1. What or who has been operable in your identity construction? What sources have you used to think about who you are?

2. When has your voice been silenced? When have you had to or wanted to speak up for one who was silenced? Who has helped you to find your voice—and keep it?

3. Develop your own core commitments worksheet. Each core commitment should include a brief summary of why it is essential for the preservation of your identity and how you will know a sense of balance in your ministry.

RESOURCES

http://revgalblogpals.org.

Mary Field Belenky, Blyth McVicker Clinchy, Nancy Rule Goldberg, and Jill Mattuck Tarule, *Women's Ways of Knowing: The Development of Self, Voice, and Mind* (New York: Basic Books, 1986).

Tina Fey, *Bossypants* (London: Little Brown, 2011).

Adam Hamilton, *Speaking Well* (Nashville: Abingdon, 2015).

Ashley-Anne Masters and Stacy Smith, *Bless Her Heart: Life as a Young Clergy Woman* (St. Louis: Chalice, 2011).

Quentin Schultze, *An Essential Guide to Public Speaking* (Grand Rapids, MI: Baker Academic, 2006).

Martha Spong, ed., *There's a Woman in the Pulpit* (Woodstock, VT: Skylight Paths, 2015).

KEY NUMBER FOUR

THE TRUTH ABOUT SEXISM

i
you
us
them
those people
wouldn't it be lovely
if one could
live
in a constant state
of we?
some of the most
commonplace
words
can be some of the biggest
dividers
they
what if there was
no they?
what if there
was only
us?
if words could be seen
as they floated out
of our mouths
would we feel no
shame
as they passed beyond
our lips?
if we were to string
our words
on a communal clothesline
would we feel proud
as our thoughts
flapped in the
breeze?
—Marilyn Maciel, "clothesline"

INTRODUCTION

Your value does not decrease based on someone's inability to see your worth.

—*Unknown*

KEY NUMBER FOUR for unlocking the power of women in ministry is to tell the truth that sexism is alive and well—especially in the church. The truth is that you will experience sexism, overtly and covertly; it is just a matter of time. If you anticipate or hope that the church is immune to the sexism you have experienced or about which you have heard and learned up to the point of considering ministry, this chapter will shatter that assumption—and it has to.

The truth about sexism in the church needs to be heard, it needs to be told, and it needs to be called out. If this chapter is not devastating to you, then it will not have accomplished its intended goal. It should be devastating that you will still experience sexism when it comes to your call to ministry. It should be devastating that the one institution on which you depend to be the most vocal about fighting sexism is the most resoundingly silent. It should be devastating that the one place where you might be able to escape the sexism of our culture will only make it worse. These facts could very well lead to discouragement. Why enter into ministry if you know that this is what you will face? Ministry is hard enough without having to prepare yourself for the many ways that sexism will succeed in demoralizing your position and sense of call.

Yet, these truths are not meant to be discouraging but to give rise to justified anger. Your anger will be justified and not only on the grounds of any one specific incident alone. It will be justified because the church should be so much better about dealing with sexism. The church, of all places, should not explain sexism away, sweep it under the rug, or insist it is really "not that bad." Your anger will be justified because you will experience little to no support from those who you thought "had your back." You will look around and say to yourself, because you can't bring yourself to say it aloud to the bystanders, "Did you just hear that? Say something!" but they will not. Your anger will be justified because sexism is something your male colleagues will not have to deal with, and yet you have to expend energy and emotion on something that should have been addressed long ago. Your anger will be justified because you will just want the comments to stop, you will want to tell someone to shut up, and all too often you will bite your tongue, because the repercussions of responding can be worse than the initial insult. Why do we bite our tongues? This is a really important question to answer. Do we feel like we have to? Is it the result of fear? What are we afraid of? Is it not worth the effort, the "fight"? Monitoring these occasions when you choose to stay silent instead of speaking into the moment is an essential strategy for dealing with the sure reality of sexism.

The inclination will be to put aside your anger, to tell yourself to "calm down," or to convince yourself that it is an overreaction, that you are too sensitive, or that you are making "too big of a deal" about it. However, there is a difference between healthy anger and self-righteous indignation. You will have every right, every single right, to be angry, to experience hurt, and to feel—truly feel—diminished and demeaned. In fact, those are all the underlying and hoped-for goals of sexism. Those reactions are exactly the ones that sexism intends to instill deep within your soul. While there will be sexist comments about you and directed to you that will come from people who "do not know any better" and who do not realize the effects that their comments might have, there will be others who know exactly what they are doing. They know the power that sexism has to bring you down and to cause you to question your performance in ministry, but more insidiously, to get you to question your very call to ministry. These persons are not capable of telling the truth about their feelings toward you and so they hide behind sexism. These concealed feelings will likely include the belief that you should not be in ministry (especially true if you are clergy). Because they are unable to utter this belief out loud, sexism becomes the means by which they can make you feel what they feel. Sexism may also mask or deflect unwanted feelings of attraction by twisting them into ridicule and degradation.

The truth about sexism in the church is that the church is not only a place where sexism is tolerated, it is actively harbored and justified. Sexism in the church lives and thrives because it can ground its reasons for un-critical acquiescence to sexism on biblical and theological bases, without even having to work particularly hard. Undoing the rampant sexism in the church, however, is more difficult; reports of sexism are even downplayed and disbelieved, because "we all mean well" in the church. No one really means to be sexist; it is just the way it is. This excuse makes it all the more difficult for you to navigate its inevitability. It becomes harder still when you are a leader in the church, whether a pastor, a minister, clergy, or a lay employee, and so of course you would never respond so unkindly as to call out sexist comments or make someone "feel bad" when they did not have any negative intentions. To take on sexism, the church would have to revise its script so drastically that it is simply not willing, or cannot face, the rewrites.

The truth is that sexism is harder to navigate as a woman in ministry than a woman in business because of the belief that we will accept these comments as unintentional and because we are expected to react even to unkindness with love. If we respond in such a way that our retorts are deemed unkind, we run the risk of all kinds of interpretive results: we are not very Christian, we are awfully sensitive, or we sound or look bitchy (as if bitchy always has to be a bad thing). For example, Resting Bitch Face (RBF). For men, a stern look is acceptable. For women, it is deemed bitchy.[1]

Alertness to and negotiation of sexism in ministry demands knowl-edge about its many and various levels, and reflection on how and when you will go about speaking up for and against the unspeakable. To be able to traverse the complicated landscape of sexism will demand wisdom concerning the nature and function of sexism, but also honesty about its effect on you. You will need to be aware of the emotions that will surface when you are the object of sexist comments. In other words, sexism is so difficult because you not only have to figure out how to reply to its particular origin at the time, but also how to respond to your own reactions in the moment.

Sexism is insidious because it—and the people who use it—know the kinds of feelings it will bring about, typically feelings tied to insecurity, self-esteem, and shame. At the same time, the emotions and reactions that surface in the moment of being the object of sexism are as complicated as you are unique. Your feelings of insecurity could be connected to your ministry or to your intellect. Your feelings of self-esteem could be associated with your body. Your feelings of shame could be linked to past abuse. In order to diminish, but never entirely eradicate the effects of sexism, some deliberation and reflection on where you stand with regard to these particular emotional manifestations will help.

This is another truth: no matter how much we give reasons for, explain, or acknowledge sexism, it will still have an effect and it will still catch you off guard. A comment in a moment when you are feeling vulnerable. A remark from someone you thought you could trust. And in the end, there is no explaining it or justifying it. Sexism just is. And sexism will continue to be.

Sexism, in this regard, is a manifestation of our human brokenness, our human propensity to find ways to exert power over the other and to bring down those who have the power we seek. Sexism is a manifestation of sin, with sin being defined as separation from God and the rejection of the emancipatory power of God's love. The farther away we are from the ways in which we know how God's power works, the less capable we are of embodying power that seeks to lift up and not bring down, that acknowledges worth in the other even in the moments when we feel the most unworthy, and that is committed to the means by which the other is valued fully in all of her individuality and femininity and not as an object for the taking.

Essential to unlocking your power as a woman in ministry is thinking about what it will take in your ministry to be proactive rather than reactive in moments when you are the target of sexism. You will need to think about how to respond to sexist comments that are harmless, where the person has absolutely no idea that they are hurtful, as well as those that are meant to hurt and cause harm. How will you respond to the most challenging issue with sexism—its perceived acceptance in our society? The excuse that boys will be boys? Men will be men?

It is not possible to contain in one book the many examples of sexism to which you will be subjected. Imagine that behind one experience, one story, lies at least a thousand more. That is not exaggeration. That is not hyperbole. That is the truth. This chapter will set out the kinds of sexism you will experience as a woman in ministry. It will provide a taxonomy, of sorts, with examples and suggestions for ways to adjudicate the remarks, maneuver the situations, but also negotiate your own feelings.

On the one hand, this is a rather dispiriting exercise in and of itself. We should not have to embark on these efforts so as to secure our success in ministry. At the same time, some calculation ahead of time will mean being in a better place to thwart those efforts that seek to undermine your success. You will not know how to respond to these situations without being able to realize the nature of the incident, its context, and what it is triggering in you.

The power of sexism and the discussion of this power, therefore, has to follow what was put forward in KEY TWO and KEY THREE of this book. Essential to negotiating the certainty of sexism in ministry is to draw on the "work" you do in thinking about KEY TWO and KEY THREE. How you are able to know and express your identity and your authenticity in both your speech and your body is linked to monitoring the sexism you will experience and your responses to it.

THE NATURE OF SEXISM

I thought about quitting but then noticed who was watching.

—*Unknown*

The truth of sexism is that it is a form of prejudice—gender prejudice. In that regard, it functions like any other means of prejudice by which, to unpack the etymology of the word, persons or groups of people are prejudged based on a certain, determined classification. Prejudice includes discrimination on the basis of race, ethnicity, age, class, sexual orientation, ability, weight, education, sickness . . . and still, this is hardly an exhaustive list.

Essential, however, to getting at the debilitating effects of sexism is beginning with some discussion of how sexism works. Sexism is not just a topic of interest in ministry, but a phenomenon in ministry, and we must take seriously its phenomenological power. Sexism is not only a thing; it is an action that, purposeful or not, is a form of abuse. The spectrum of sexism, of course, falls along the lines named above. There is sexism that is benign, in which the perpetrator has simply no idea of what he, or sometimes she, has done. These comments are easily rolled off the back; "Oh, that's just John. He always says stuff like that." But at the other end of the sexism spectrum is an act of sexism that knows exactly what it is doing. It has every intent of belittling and objectifying who you are as a woman. In part, therefore, one of the more exhausting realities of sexism is this constant need to interpret what kind of sexism you are experiencing and how it makes you feel.

This is a very real circumstance of being a woman in ministry that your male colleagues will never, ever have to contend with, and they will not understand, as much as they might want to try, or think that they can. Your male colleagues are not your sources of support in these circumstances, although your gay friends will have a better sense of it and transgender men will get it because many of them have experienced it firsthand. At the same time, however, your male colleagues can be your advocates by calling out sexism when it occurs. Before this can happen, however, you will need to be your own advocate: you will need to have this most difficult conversation with your male colleagues, probably more than once, to make sure that they are aware of the reality of sexism in the church and their own complicity in it.

A GLOSSARY OF SEXISM

Unlocking the power of being a woman in ministry means knowing your sexism vocabulary. It means that you are familiar with the various forms that sexism takes and how it manifests itself so that you are able to diagnose the particular "brand" of sexism with which you are having to cope. In addition to this dictionary of standard sexism terms, you will also need to have an awareness of various neologisms so as to negotiate and navigate the kinds of sexism you will experience. Consider this a glossary for women in ministry (all definitions at http://www.merriam-webster .com unless otherwise noted).

Sexual Harassment (as defined by the United States Equal Opportunity Employment Program): "It is unlawful to harass a person (an applicant or employee) because of that person's sex. Harassment can include 'sexual harassment' or unwelcome sexual advances, requests for sexual favors, and other verbal or physical harassment of a sexual nature. Harassment does not have to be of a sexual nature, however, and can include offensive remarks about a person's sex. For example, it is illegal to harass a woman by making offensive comments about women in general. Both victim and the harasser can be either a woman or a man, and the victim and harasser can be the same sex. Although the law doesn't prohibit simple teasing, offhand comments, or isolated incidents that are not very serious, harassment is illegal when it is so frequent or severe that it creates a hostile or offensive work environment or when it results in an adverse employment decision (such as the victim being fired or demoted). The harasser can be the victim's supervisor, a supervisor in another area, a co-worker, or someone who is not an employee of the employer, such as a client or customer."[2]

Consider this example:

> "Last week, on three separate occasions, I was verbally harassed by complete strangers regarding me being a female clergy. I mean, people yelling at me from across the street. One man followed me for three blocks and then started to threaten sexual violence in order to 'straighten me out' because 'women shouldn't have authority over men.' It got to be so threatening that I had to duck into a restaurant to get away."

Sexism: "unfair treatment of people because of their sex; *especially* : unfair treatment of women." The following examples were shared by pastors:

"At annual meeting: I wore a tweed (!) dress and black blazer. I was told that I should disrobe (verbatim, and intentionally) more often on Sunday mornings so that people could 'enjoy' what's under the robe."

"Man: If I had had a pastor like you when I was a teenager, I would have never missed church. (After worship while standing by the chancel.)"

"That moment when you have a creepy old guy in your congregation who constantly remarks upon your looks…yep, that guy is still in my congregation and told me today how horrible I look recently and that I should 'pretty myself up so he can enjoy looking at me again.'"

Feminism: "the belief that men and women should have equal rights and opportunities." One of the common remarks that will be lodged against you is the label of "feminist," particularly if you choose to lift up women's rights, speak about the plight and perils of women in the Bible, or use feminine imagery for God. To be a feminist is then in the same camp as an ideologue. You must have a particular agenda that you are now attempting to force on others. This misunderstanding of feminism is still present and it may mean that you will need to demonstrate and talk about what true feminism is.

Patriarchy: "social organization marked by the supremacy of the father in the clan or family, the legal dependence of wives and children, and the reckoning of descent and inheritance in the male line; *broadly*: control by men of a disproportionately large share of power."

Androcentrism: "dominated by or emphasizing masculine interests or a masculine point of view."

Misogyny: "a hatred of women."

Rape Culture: "a complex set of beliefs that encourage male sexual aggression and supports violence against women. It is a society where violence is seen as sexy and sexuality as violent. In a rape culture, women perceive a continuum of threatened violence that ranges from sexual remarks to sexual touching to rape itself. A rape culture condones physical and emotional terrorism against women as the norm...In a rape culture both men and women assume that sexual violence is a fact of life, inevitable....However...much of what we accept as inevitable is in fact the expression of values and attitudes that can change.

"Rape culture includes jokes, TV, music, advertising, legal jargon, laws, words and imagery that make violence against women and sexual coercion seem so normal that people believe that rape is inevitable. Rather than viewing the culture of rape as a problem to change, people in a rape culture think about the persistence of rape as 'just the way things are.'"[3]

Ambivalent Sexism: the theory that sexism is actually executed by means of two differing types of sexism: hostile sexism and benevolent sexism. "Hostile sexism is an adversarial view of gender relations in which women are perceived as seeking to control men, whether through sexuality or feminist ideology." Benevolent sexism "recognizes that some forms of sexism are, for the perpetrator, subjectively benevolent, characterizing women as pure creatures who ought to be protected, supported, and adored and whose love is necessary to make a man complete." Benevolent sexism appears as it sounds—the woman is cherished, but "it serves as a crucial compliment to hostile sexism that helps to pacify women's resistance to societal gender inequality."[4] The problem with benevolent sexism is that it "sounds so darn friendly."[5] Yet, it is insidiously present and perpetuates stereotypes of women and male dominance. One pastor who served a church with her husband was being considered for a new call. When she did not get the call, she was told that the reason she was not offered the position was because "you and your husband clearly have a positive ministry that we would not want to break up." Translated, the call committee told her "we're not sure you can do ministry without your man."

Sexist Microaggressions: "the everyday verbal, nonverbal, and environmental slights, snubs, or insults, whether intentional or unintentional, which communicate hostile, derogatory, or negative messages to target persons based solely upon their marginalized group membership."[6]

Additional reflection on and consideration of sexist microaggressions is critical as a woman in ministry. It is these "everyday" communications, as discussed above on the effect of rhetoric, that have the overall consequence of simply wearing you down. Furthermore, the impact of the microaggressions lies not only in the message itself but the "hidden meaning" behind the message. "These hidden messages may invalidate the group identity or experiential reality of target persons, demean them on a personal or group level, communicate they are lesser human beings, suggest they do not belong with the majority group, threaten and intimidate, or relegate them to inferior status and treatment."[7] Consider the following examples:

An assertive female manager is labeled as a "bitch," while her male counterpart is described as "a forceful leader." (Hidden message: Women should be passive and allow men to be the decision makers.) A female physician wearing a stethoscope is mistaken as a nurse. (Hidden message: Women should occupy nurturing and not decision-making roles. Women are less capable than men.) Whistles or catcalls are heard from men as a woman walks down the street. (Hidden message: Your body/appearance is for the enjoyment of men. You are a sex object.)[8]

Applying this reality to the circumstances you will encounter as a woman in ministry is essential. For example, one pastor shared, "I've had a receptionist at a Catholic hospital refuse to give me a token to leave their parking lot because I couldn't possibly be a minister." In her blog, Emily Meyer shares that her ordination was delayed because her candidacy committee thought she was "overly assertive." In their words, "Your results are what we'd hope to see in a promising male candidate; but as a female they raise some red flags."[9] In a discussion about jewelry and clothing, one pastor shared a time she was critiqued for wearing dangly earrings while preaching. The hidden message that surfaced in the subsequent conversation was that not only were they distracting, but that "a lot of 'distraction' complaints seem more like 'I can't handle my sexual impulses and think that's your problem' sentiments."

Mansplaining: when a man talks condescendingly to someone (especially a woman) about something of which he has incomplete knowledge, with the mistaken assumption that he knows more about it than the person to whom he is talking. The following is an example from a pastor.

"Last night I preached and presided at a memorial service for a 58-year-old man who died of an aggressive form of cancer. The family wanted to invite anyone to share stories about him during the service (usually I try to get families to have a couple of specific stories picked out in advance, but this family insisted that they wanted any and all to speak). I chose to preach prior to the story sharing to try to get things rolling with theology grounded in God's love and grace including:

- this isn't fair, he should be with us, death isn't fair, it's horrible
- God didn't do this, God didn't take him, God doesn't do bad things to his people
- resurrection, resurrection, resurrection, promises we have and the deceased has
- we can be sad and angry about this, but be assured that death doesn't win

"And then...third story into it all, a male (mid-50s) friend of the family stood up and said to the 250+ people gathered, "I disagree with your pastor here. She has some nice thoughts, but she's wrong." ... He went on to explain that there were grace and blessings at the end of the deceased life. I do not disagree with this at all. ... I thought I preached the Good News, but apparently because I didn't say it the way he wanted to hear it, I was simply wrong. I just can't believe he called me out like that ... he's not even one of my members or super close to the family ... and what could I do but smile and let it be? I know it's God's house, but all I could think was "how dare you come into my house and do such a thing?!?"

Bropropriation: "taking a woman's idea and taking credit for it."[10]
Manterrupting: "unnecessary interruption of a woman by a man."[11]

The ability to name the kind of sexism you are experiencing goes a long way toward figuring out how you want to handle a given situation. At the very least, it names it for what it is, and calls it out for the truth that it tries to hide. That naming, that acknowledging of its presence and existence, is a direct countermeasure to the name-calling on which sexism relies. There is power in that moment of naming it, bringing it out into the open for all to see. It can then no longer abscond its real motivations. It can then no longer veil its intent to harm. You have undermined its power with your power in telling the truth.

THE RHETORIC OF SEXISM

"In fact, if you don't speak up at this very important time, relief and rescue will appear for the Jews from another place, but you and your family will die. But who knows? Maybe it was for a moment like this that you came to be part of the royal family."

—Esther 4:14

Dealing with sexism necessitates a basic knowledge of how communication works and what it does. Figuring out how to deal with sexism, then, requires a nuanced comprehension of the origins and consequences of basic rhetoric. While rhetoric in this day and age has gained a pejorative reputation, rhetoric in the classical sense is an art form. Of course, one of the best examples of the power of rhetoric is the Bible itself. The authors of the New Testament books, in particular, write for the ear and not for the eye. They draw on basic techniques of classical rhetoric so as to communicate effectively and persuade their audiences of a message. Paul himself was trained in rhetoric and he used it not only to convince but also to move the minds and hearts of his listeners from one place to another.

Rhetorical language is designed to have an effect on the audience. The craft of speaking acknowledges the effectiveness of rhetoric and knows how to use it efficiently. In classical rhetoric, the definition of a rhetorician is one who senses the poignancy of the moment and is able to speak into it. In other words, a rhetorician has the tools in place to address a situation because she has the ability to read the tone of the moment, what the audience needs to hear, and what needs to be said. A rhetorician, a public speaker, and a preacher know that it is not just what you say but how you say it. Words do not just say things. Words do things. The narrative mode—the genre, the techniques, all of the rhetorical skills available—communicate meaning as much as the content or material itself.

When it comes to communication and the primary functions and purposes of rhetoric, it is helpful to remember on what rhetoric is grounded: the rhetorical triangle. Ancient rhetoric is situated in the premise of a triangle of *logos*, *pathos*, and *ethos*. *Logos* refers to the subject matter being presented or communicated, of which the speaker wants to persuade the audience. Of course, for the New Testament authors, their *logos* is not just subject matter but the Word made flesh, Jesus Christ. The *ethos* refers to the speaker. Ancient rhetoric anticipates that the speaker, in the speaking, reveals her or his character. Critical to the success of persuasion is whether or not the character can be believed. What you say and how you say it reveals who you are. The *ethos* in rhetoric notes the element of choice in the entirety of the proclaimed message. Think about political campaigns. In the speeches of the candidates, you are listening not only for their message, but you are also assessing the nature of their character. You are trying to find out about the person—who they are, what they stand for, what is important to them. What you say reveals who you are. How you communicate also lets people know what is at stake for you.

The third point on the triangle is *pathos*. The *pathos* is the audience. The speaker has to know the audience to be effective. You need to know your audience as well as you know yourself and as well as you know your subject matter. As discussed above, your audience will be able to tell what you think about them. If you have not tended to the nature, the make up of the audience and its contexts, and the situation to which the audience assumes you will speak, the chances of your message being communicated or having the effect you intended will be compromised.

All three angles of the rhetorical triangle are not only essential for assessing the effects of communication; they also help to understand why the rhetoric of sexism is all the more difficult and disempowering. To experience sexism is first to locate yourself as the "audience," the *pathos* of the argument or statement being made. As a result, the sexism you experience puts you in the place of the audience who realizes that the speaker has not spent the necessary time getting to know the audience. You detect the oversight of familiarizing yourself with the listeners, especially true in the case of unintentional sexism. In the other case, the speaker has, indeed, familiarized himself, but with the intent to cause harm. The fact that the person charged with sexism has not fully realized his audience makes the effects of the sexism, intended or not, all the more hurtful. Your role as a listener, as an audience, is diminished, as is who you are as a woman. It has the double effect of disempowering and demeaning. There is no difference between the experience of a collective audience, and the experience of an individual, who has known this indifference to their situation.

To face sexism from the perspective of the *logos* is to realize the possibility that what is being communicated, the subject matter, is actually believed by the speaker. This may not be an accidental comment or a nonchalant statement, but has the potential to be a thought-out argument, a declaration that hopes for an intended effect, and an allegation that makes a very certain claim about who you are. If the subject matter, the *logos*, is that which the speaker wishes to communicate, then in the case of sexism, the hoped-for communication is that your gender makes you less and that who you are as a woman is deserving of discrimination, of being considered socially second-tier, and of being objectified.

To be the recipient of sexism, and consider the meaning and function of *ethos* in the rhetorical triangle, is to have the devastating realization of having to reorient your relationship with the person speaking. If the *ethos* assumes the manifestation of character, what the person communicates cannot necessarily be differentiated from the speaker's own beliefs and commitments. An experience of sexism changes relationship because it changes how you feel about the person by whom you have been demeaned. It sets in motion the necessity to reevaluate and recalibrate what you have known or thought about the person. It requires a reconstruction of trust and of vulnerability.

To unlock the power of being a woman in ministry necessitates being an observer of rhetoric. This means listening for the ways in which sexism is played out—not only for you and your colleagues in your particular ministry settings—but also in our society, both nationally and globally. You will need to be conscious about the way in which sexism is an absolute and determined means by which people communicate with and to women, so that you recognize the truth of its ubiquity and realize you are not alone. This consciousness is also necessary for the sake of the women to whom you minister. Your complacency, silence, or unwillingness to give voice to the effect of sexism on you suggests to those in your congregation that it is acceptable for them to tolerate in their work or home.

One of your charges as a woman in ministry, as a leader in the church, is to communicate to other women that sexism is unacceptable. Period. It is an expression of your personal power to stop hurtful behavior. While your strongest impulse might be to ignore it, brush it aside, pretend that it did not happen, or convince yourself that it is no big deal, you will have parishioners (both women and men) watching this behavior and then assuming that such actions are acceptable. The men will then surmise that you do not care, that it is all in fun, that you can "take a joke," and that it does not seem to bother you, and the sexism will continue, and perhaps even increase in its frequency and intensity. Women will deduce that a woman's role in the church is to accept these comments; that the church, even according to its scripture, presupposes that this treatment of women is tolerable, even normal.

As a woman in ministry, you certainly have accountability to yourself when it comes to sexism. You will have to be responsible for your own self-protection because when it comes to sexism, few will stand up for you. You will have to listen to how it feels and honor your feelings. People remain on the sidelines of sexism because they assume the interchange is personal. As with conflict, they do not want to get involved and they do not know what to say. People also have a general discomfort with sexism because they do not know how to deal with the perceived or possible sexual tension they witness or experience themselves. But the more unnerving reason for this passivity is that sexism is an acceptable form of communication in our culture. It is so pervasive that we do not notice it. It has become a larger context that we are unable to see and therefore is far more difficult to critique. As a woman in ministry, your responsibility is not only for yourself, but for others, to help them see what they cannot see: that sexism has become a commonplace part of communication, particularly in the church. Yet, it needs to be the church, in which you are a leader, that tells the truth about what sexism is and what sexism does.

Part of our calling as women in ministry is to encourage women and girls in whom we see potential for vocations in ministry. We need to identify those women, perhaps as you were, who have gifts for ministry, and encourage them to consider a call in the church. Yet, if they observe passivity in us when it comes to sexism, particularly as it plays out in the church, to what extent will we have become a deterrent to their imagination as having a future in ministry, rather than an advocate for them? If they see in us an acceptance of sexism as "just the way it is," will they then determine that they do not want to be a part of a church like that? If we lead Bible studies on women in the scriptures, or preach sermon series that elevate the voices of women, but do not call out sexism in our own contexts, will women who are considering calls turn away in disgust at our hypocrisy? If they do not view in us someone who is willing to work toward the transformation of the church, have we succeeded in communicating that the church is beyond the capability of being transformed, or that it is not worth the effort to do so?

As a result, in addition to the extraordinary difficulty of dealing with sexism on a personal level, we are dealing with the hard work of negotiating sexism for the sake of the other. Standing up against sexism for the sake of the wholeness of the other—for the wholeness of the church— means risk, and it also means a most certain absence of reciprocity. Standing up against sexism for the sake of the other will necessarily contribute to the loneliness that ministry itself tends to create. Much of this work, both the protection of yourself and the protection of the other, will have to happen from your own place of power. You will have to risk how your power is perceived for the sake of change and for the sake of creating safe spaces for other women to be in church and to be church.

An essential strategy for navigating sexism in its varied forms is to keep a sexism log. Keeping a log for one week will suffice to bring to the surface the variations of sexism you will experience. Important to the success of this exercise is to chart even those comments that you want to write off as "that's not really sexism" or "I'm not really sure, so I will give that person the benefit of the doubt" or "that wasn't that bad, was it?" You will want to make excuses that either exonerate the perpetrator or blame yourself. In order to get the most accurate results of this exercise, and to deflect those who would say that you are manipulating results to make sexism worse than it is, you need to document every possible instance, and adjudicate later whether or not comments were actually a form of sexism. In all likelihood, they all will be forms of sexism; we just do not want that to be the truth. Denial is powerful and it functions very well on both sides of how sexism plays out. You will find yourself denying its prevalence, wanting to find excuses to make it better than it is. Others will want to deny its pervasiveness, either because they do not want to believe it or they begin to wonder if they themselves have perpetuated it. The most productive approach to a log of this nature is to chart the incident, the source, the setting, and give a brief description of your reaction or explanation of your feelings. Being able to describe how it makes you feel is a vital aspect of this exercise because the feelings that result from sexism are sexism's intended goal.

Do you feel anger? One pastor shared, "I saw this book (*Femmevangelical: The Modern Girl's Guide to the Good News*) on my SP's (supervising pastor) desk and told him how excited I was he had bought it and that I am really enjoying reading it. Then he called me 'sweetheart' and said he bought it for the cover. Then turned to the other AP (associate pastor) and said, 'How about we make a new associate position we can offer to a pastor who dresses like this?' I'm furious with myself for not saying anything. And also overwhelmed with the irony of the conversation."

Do you feel blame? Shame? Do you feel demoralized? Do you feel uneasy, even in danger? If you find yourself in a position where you think you are the victim of sexual harassment, documentation is absolutely essential. But another critical benefit of this exercise is to begin to realize how much sexism is a part of our daily lives and to realize the extent to which we have simply come to the point of being able to ignore it or, worse, not even see that it is there. The omnipresence of sexism renders it invisible and is, in part, why it is still acceptable. It is part of the fabric of our lives. Sexism is one of those things that when you start seeing it, it is everywhere. Even rather innocent terms used all the time, such as "you guys" or "grandfathered in" contribute to the ways in which sexism is embedded in our speech. To be able to call it out and give voice to the truth of its effects on how we see ourselves and how we do ministry, we have to be able to see its commonness. We cannot articulate or even accept how much sexism is interwoven into the rhetoric of our lives without charting its instances.

THE EFFECTS OF RHETORIC

The worse you think you're doing, the less likely you are to ask for help.

—*Brené Brown*

While there are many and sundry techniques, tools, and skills available to the rhetorician, perhaps the one most effective, particularly when it comes to sexism, is repetition. Repetition works toward multiple results. First, it is an essential property for achieving memory. Memory is critical for communication that ends up attaining an intended result because the subject matter you have communicated lasts beyond the moment of communication. Few will be affected by what you say if they cannot remember what you said. At the same time, a memory has a lasting effect. Our ability to recall vividly a moment of trauma, where, for instance, we have experienced the objectification of sexism, needs only the smallest of triggers. In other words, the power of sexism is its effect beyond the moment itself. For example, a childhood taunt has the potential to resurface in an occurrence of sexism. An event will come crashing forward and even be reexperienced when the sexist comment succeeds in generating the memory. We need to be fully aware that the pithy phrase "sticks and stones may break my bones but names will never hurt me" is, perhaps, one of the greatest untruths. Names hurt deeply, intensely, and they are experiences that you really never get over or beyond. Sexism depends on memory. It relies on the fact that a comment made today will recall a painful moment in your past. It intends that the pain of the past will contribute to the pain of the present. And it succeeds—every single time.

Sexism also truncates your future. It triumphs in abbreviating your imagination for what you are called to do and who you can be. It thrives on setting parameters for your identity, limits to your abilities, and restrictions to your own potential. It knows how quickly we can let our past determine our future. It realizes our insecurities, seeks out our flaws, and preys on our deepest vulnerabilities. It counts on our desire for affirmation in its false affirmation. It banks on our need to feel worthy by making the basis of our worth rest entirely upon how we look. It is fully aware of how difficult it is to embody our true selves, and looks for any crack in the surface by which to replace authenticity with illusion.

Second, repetition is a necessary element for realizing an intended effect. The more you hear something said, the more it weighs on you, and the more you believe it. If you are told over and over again that you are stupid, fat, and unworthy, you eventually come to believe that truth. The power of repetition is not simply to make a point but to create the experience of the point, which can be felt in both positive and negative ways. Four examples may help to demonstrate this phenomenon.

On the Twin Cities campus of the University of Minnesota is the Weisman Art Museum. Described as a "teaching" museum, its mission "creates art experiences that spark discovery, critical thinking, and transformation, linking the University and the community."[12] Toward the end of the 2008 United States presidential campaign, the museum sponsored an exhibit by artist R. Luke Dubois titled "Hindsight Is Always 20/20." Dubois describes his project:

> HINDSIGHT IS ALWAYS 20/20 takes the State of the Union addresses from each presidency and sorts them according to word frequency, generating a Snellen eye chart for each president, with the more frequent words in larger typeface at the top of the chart and the less frequent words towards the bottom. The 66-member word lists for each presidency are designed to draw out the most unique and contemporary vocabulary used by the

president in his speeches; words that appear in the majority of speeches (e.g. "united," "states," "the," "his," "her," "am") are cancelled out; words that appear in a few Presidents' speeches are given to the President who uses the word the most. As a result, the list contains words that are not only important in a given presidency but also au courant in terms of lexicon and contemporary context.

The aim of the piece is to make a statement about the perennial political metaphor of vision, without which much of the rhetoric of presidential politics quickly deflates. The choice of words employed by a given presidential administration to articulate its message is in many ways its signature. Looking back, we can use this vocabulary to test the metaphorical eyesight of the nation throughout its history.[13]

The visual result of Dubois's project illustrates the aural effect of repetition. As Dubois notes, the word most repeated is the word placed at the top of the chart. Visually, this is stunning. But when listening to the speech, the effect of hearing that one word over and over again is emotionally profound. The point of the repetition is not only to carry the primary point or message of the speech, but to create the sensation of the word that is being repeated. The word most repeated in Abraham Lincoln's State of the Union address was "emancipation." The word most repeated in George W. Bush's address after the September 11, 2001, attack on the World Trade Center in New York City was "terror." In other words, Lincoln wished for his listeners to feel emancipated. Bush wanted the American people to feel terror.

The second example to illuminate the impact of repetition in communication is Martin Luther King Jr.'s "I Have a Dream" speech. Were Dubois to sort King's speech for word frequency, the word that would appear at the top of the chart would be "freedom." "Freedom" was not only the primary topic of King's speech but he wanted those 250,000 people listening to experience freedom. A rhetorical analysis of the "I Have a Dream" speech reveals no fewer than a half dozen known rhetorical devices in every single paragraph. King brought home the importance of freedom, the feeling of freedom, at the end of the speech with his use of *anaphora*: the repetition of a word or phrase at the beginning of several successive clauses. The phrase King used to close out the address was "let freedom ring." The effect is remarkable in how it quite literally created the jubilation and celebration of knowing freedom at last.

A third example of the effect of repetition in speech, communication, and relationship is the permanent exhibit at the Museum of Tolerance in Los Angeles, California (referenced in chapter 1), called the "Tunnel of Prejudice." Museum patrons walk through this tunnel as slurs are called out. The experience of a "tunnel of oppression" has been replicated on college campuses in the United States. The purpose of the tunnel is to create the experience of what it is like to be the object of discrimination, marginalization, and even violence. The emotional effect of this exhibit is shocking. You start to realize the unexpected afterlife of the comments, slurs, and insults. Perhaps some you can shrug off, and you wonder why that is the case, because others find their way deep into your psyche, where self-doubt and insecurity abide. They become internalized to the extent that they then become believable. And then, there are those remarks where you recognize that in different circumstances, like walking home alone after dark, they are precursors of violence. The potential threat of physical harm, the palpability of fear, the sense of danger caused by one word in the right place stops you in your tracks.

The final example of how repetition works comes from the Bible. The reason any interpreter of scripture engages in concordance work when doing biblical exegesis is to discover what words are important and unique to the biblical authors. Concordance work also locates particular placement of words, which is also meant to have an effect on the experience of a given work, and which contributes to potential meaning, and meanings, in interpretation. In the case of repetition, the Gospel of John is an excellent example of the repetition of a word both to create and emphasize theological meaning, but with a positive result, unlike the examples above. In the Fourth Gospel, this word is "abide" (Greek, *menō*). This term, translated in the Gospel of John into English as "abide, remain, stay, continue" is used over forty times in the narrative. It is the central theological claim of the Gospel of John, the mutual abiding between God, Jesus, and the believer, and is the primary description of relationship. As a result, the repetition of the word "abide" not only communicates the main point of the Gospel but also creates the experience of what it feels like to abide in the Word, and that abiding in the Word, then, means an intimate relationship with Jesus—and with God.

These four examples call attention to the ways by which repetition as a basic element of rhetoric and communication has profound consequences. Repetition can be a vehicle for positive affirmation and attention, but also has the capability of securing any opposite effect. In experiences of sexism, repetition has the result of emphasizing the marginalization, diminishment, and discrimination already inherent in the words themselves to an even greater measure. Sexism depends on the power of rhetoric to ensure that the chosen words do as much damage as possible.

CHANGING HOW WE TALK

What we speak becomes the house we live in.

—*Hafiz*

The power of words resides also, of course, in the words themselves. Word choices matter, how we speak matters, and unlocking the power of being a woman in ministry necessitates that you tend these choices carefully. This tending begins with observation. We listen to the language of others when it comes to women and we listen to our own language when we express what it means to be a woman and a woman in ministry. Of tremendous import, when it comes to the power of rhetoric and sexism, is the surveillance of your own speech.

How we talk matters. When we begin this talk matters even more. Consider, for example, the way we talk to little girls.[14] The first comments we have been socialized to make revolve around appearance—the cuteness of the dress, outfit, shoes, or hair—rather than about her mind or her interests, which are topics we reserve for little boys. If we, as adult women, perpetuate this kind of role-talk when addressing little girls, imagine what men, young men, and boys assume to be appropriate. Why should they speak to us in ways that we do not even speak to one another?

There are several examples that are helpful to consider when it comes to assessing the vocabulary we observe, use, and assume in expressing our power as women in ministry. While it is true that women's speech is over-policed and overgeneralized,[15] the point here is to consider your own ways of self-expression. Critical to our own sense of power as women in ministry is mindfulness of how we articulate our thoughts, ideas, and beliefs. Observations around language use—that women tend to be self-diminutive, say *just* too much, apologize too frequently, and allow themselves to be interrupted—are generalizations. They can be helpful if you survey your own speech, discover these patterns, and find that they do not align with who you know yourself to be. Generalizations are, however, only helpful to a certain extent, because they can easily fall into the stereotypes we are trying to outlive. For example, while the use of the word *just* may communicate uncertainty and a lack of confidence, it can also be an expression of empathy. "Even when 'just' does function as a hedge, the effect isn't necessarily to make the speaker sound unconfident."[16] Context matters considerably in all communication. At the same time, an honest assessment of your own self-expression is essential, not for the sake of excessive self-censoring, but for the sake of whether or not the language you use is an expression of your true self, identity, and authenticity. It is also to make you aware that other persons are assessing your speech and may very well have in mind these generalizations as their interpretive foundation.

Another means by which to consider the role of sexism in the church is the language we use for God. We betray our own biases, theological and gendered, when our primary references to God are male. If your own references to God are predominantly male, you intimate that thinking about God in this principal category is not only acceptable but normative. It is difficult to communicate or to convince others that women in ministry are essential to the vision of God's church when you maintain presentations and articulations of God determined by patriarchy and white, male, Anglo-Saxon interpreters.

This focused conversation on your responsibility and accountability when it comes to communication may seem unfair. This is exhausting work when ministry is already enervating. Why should we constantly have to tend our speech and the speech of others? Why can't others speak on our behalf and be our advocates? Because if we do not speak up, others will not. This will seem like a bit of an overstatement, but it is not. If it were going to happen organically, it would have happened by now. It will not happen on its own, especially in the church. The church already lags twenty years behind the trends of society and culture. To unlock your power as a woman in ministry is to claim your power to ensure transformation and change when it comes to the pervasiveness of sexism in the church.

The most difficult truth in all of this is that language is difficult to change. Words are reflective of self-expression, identity, and truth. To change how we speak means having to change, at some level, who we are. We might even wonder if how we talk is harder to change than how we act. To what extent is our behavior more easily modified than our speech because our words are revelatory of our souls? Our behavior can be written off as momentary, impulsive, or impetuous, and so has the potential to be restrained in the next instance. But our words? They are harder to explain, harder to take back. Our actions seem more readily apt to excuses than our utterances.

One of the absolute essential truths of thriving as a woman in ministry is to have girlfriends who are also in ministry. While girlfriends are absolutely essential in the whole of your ministry, they are perhaps the most critical when it comes to dealing with sexism. You will need to know that you are not alone. You will need to be affirmed in the fact that you are not making this stuff up. You will need spaces to cry, be angry, scream, and swear. Your male colleagues will not understand the cumulative consequences that sexism will have on your abilities and even your motivations to carry out the responsibilities of your call. If you have a husband or a boyfriend, he will not understand. If you are gay, and partnered, your partner will likely have some sense of what you are experiencing. There will be women in the church, *women* in the church, who think that you are an oversensitive, irrational feminist. There will be women also in ministry who will tell you this because it is how they have survived the "Old Boys Network." This is a reality of being a woman in ministry that only you and your girlfriends will know. You need girlfriends, real girlfriends. These times that you spend with them are spaces of escape, safety, and sanity. You have to know that you are not crazy. They are also spaces to complain and to vent. But in the end, they also have to be generative spaces that give you just enough so that you can return to your call, think about strategic initiatives, and review your tools for coping. Girlfriends in ministry know who you truly are and remind you of your truth.

THE MANY VARIETIES OF SEXISM

One of the most disturbing truths about sexism is its potential for serious spiritual, emotional, psychological, and physical harm. The truth about sexism is that it leads to sexual harassment, justifies domestic violence, and exacerbates rape culture. As a woman in ministry, you are both an advocate for women who suffer sexual violence and a potential victim of it. You will have women come to you with stories of sexism that have led to situations of abuse of every sort. You are, yourself, a possible victim of sexual harassment. Your position as a woman in ministry does not protect you from this possibility. And you have to know the systems in place to report it, either for yourself or for another.

The truth is, however, that the church has a dismal history of dealing with sexual harassment. With the stakes high for its self-preservation and reputation, perpetrating clergy are regularly explained and excused. The primary incident itself causes irreparable harm. The secondary harm not to be taken lightly is also the wear on your spiritual health and your own sense of call. It is no accident that the retention rates for women in ministry are far less than for men, and a central contributing fact to that statistic is the fact that sexism goes relatively unchecked in the church.

However you categorize the degrees of sexism you will experience—from minor to blatant—you will need to be aware and have others around you to corroborate when perceived acceptable sexism has crossed the line. All sexism crosses the line, of course, by its own function and definition. When we assert that there is an acceptable sexism, it continues to secure its place of influence in our lives and in our ministry. There is no acceptable sexism, but sexism continues to work because it masks itself as complimentary.

-141-

Yet there has to be a line drawn in the sand, and that is, perhaps, one of the more devastating truths of how sexism works. That line from what you can endure to what is illegal will vary. The space between tolerable and unlawful is a painful place to reside, and yet it is where all women in ministry will live. But we draw a line past which sexism is no longer tolerable: when sexism has become sexual harassment. That line marks the shift from sexism that is hurtful to sexism that is harmful and frightening. You simply have to know ahead of time the processes and systems in place that will protect you and your parishioners. What are the processes that are set out for reporting sexual harassment? What are they in your church? In your synodical bodies or judicatories? What are they in the larger institutional structures of your denomination?

One pastor shared,

I was 26, interning at a nationally prominent church, and a beloved retired minister was back visiting one Sunday. I'd never met him. Somehow, before worship, we ran into each other in the church offices, which were empty for some reason. I introduced myself. He was kind at first, and then VERY weirdly started stroking my cheek. This man, probably fifty years my senior, whom I'd never met, was touching my face in a lingering, intimate way. Can you imagine that happening to a male intern? I got very flustered and excused myself. Later, I tried to talk about it with my supervisor, the associate minister, a gay man. He literally just laughed and said, "That doesn't sound like (minister's name)!" And that was it. I'm still surprised (a) it happened and (b) my supervisor was so totally unwilling to engage with my discomfort. All from people who should theoretically know better being in the 21st-century progressive church.

While you can certainly hope that this is something you will never experience, hope is not a promise. Furthermore, it will likely be something that someone in your location of ministry is facing, and she will come to you for help. If you are in a church, it may be a parishioner or even the friend of a parishioner. If you are in a teaching institution, it will be your students who come to you with stories of sexism and, potentially, sexual harassment. These stories will have taken place in the church, on mission trips, in ecumenical gatherings, in Bible studies, and in small groups.

They will have taken place in the classroom, cafeteria, field placements, contextual education sites, and on internships. Those who have experienced sexism will come to you not only because they sense you are a safe person to whom to tell their stories, but also because they think you can do something about it. When you are open and honest about the truth of sexism, when you are doing ministry from your place of truth, you will have people coming out of the proverbial woodwork to tell their stories, knowing that you are trustworthy.

OTHER TRUTHS ABOUT SEXISM

Another way sexism thrives in the church is how it is yoked with other "isms." It can then mask itself as something else, thereby eluding address and exacerbating the other "ism" to which it is tied. This is, in part, how it continues to be acceptable and how it gets away with what it does. One of these "isms" that is particular for being a woman in ministry is ageism. While ageism describes prejudice toward older adults, ageism takes on additional meaning when it comes to women in ministry. For women in ministry who are in their forties and fifties, sexism and ageism pair together toward opinions, assumptions, and comments that have to do with menopause and menstruation, with being past their prime (in looks), and with being overlooked. Furthermore, women in ministry in their forties and fifties, while by virtue of their experience should be considered for senior positions in ministry, such as senior pastor calls, still find themselves in associate positions because the church is "not ready for a female senior pastor." Women in ministry at this age where this is a second career move have other issues that will surface for them. If they have had a family, and even grandchildren, they will immediately be cast in a "mothering" mode. As noted in chapter 3, the expectation will be that you have ministry skills in pastoral care and children and family ministry, but not as much for teaching, preaching, and administrative tasks in the church, no matter where your focus in ministry has been throughout your career.

For women in ministry who are young, the comments center around presuppositions of inexperience. Young women in ministry frequently hear comments like "Are you really old enough to be a pastor?" or "You are too cute to be a pastor," which are much rarely said to a young male, even a fresh-out-of-seminary, first-call pastor. One pastor shared, "When you have 5 visitors in worship (out of 65 in attendance) and you find out that one of your elders spoke to at least 2 of them and said, 'You'll have to excuse our pastor. She's young. She's still learning' before worship even started..." The sexism in this case hides behind youth.

As was mentioned earlier, young women in ministry who are just getting married are assumed to be less stable in their calls because their husbands' careers will take priority or because they will choose to stay at home part-time or full-time with their children. Youth and inexperience can also be a foil when it comes to recognizing and reporting sexism; young women in ministry are treated like the daughters or granddaughters of their parishioners, encouraged to accept hugs and other instances of physical intimacy as "familial" or "paternal," even when uncomfortable or blatantly sexist. Often, it is older women in ministry who resist labeling these instances as sexism or harassment, so as not to have to examine their own levels of tolerance with such behavior, their own complicity within a sexist system. The age and inexperience of the younger woman is blamed for the discomfort, rather than the act of sexism itself.

NOT JUST COPING

One acute challenge of negotiating sexism is the levels of specificity that are present in each individual situation. Each circumstance presents itself with a number of issues that also have to be addressed, in addition to the sexism itself. Responding to sexism perpetrated by an individual takes on different conditions depending on your relationship with the perpetrator. When the person is someone you have never met and with whom you have no future, it is much easier to dismiss the sexist comment and let it go. Is it really worth your comment? Is the person really worth your address? Is the exchange worth your time by extending it or your effort and energy by calling it out? The letting go can take on a number of forms. It can be a polite nod, a changing of the subject, or the nonverbal walking away. And it can be the very verbal comeback you scream in your head: "You are an idiot. Sexism is stupid. Stop it right now." It can also be a situation that is easier to call out because there are fewer repercussions.

An incident of sexism presents more difficulty when it comes from an individual with whom you have a past and a present. That moment necessitates not only adjudicating your response but also assessing on what that past and present relationship is based—and whether you want there to be a future for that relationship. Assessing that past and present relationship also helps to determine the nature of the sexist comment, like where it is coming from and why it is being said in this moment. Oftentimes, these are the comments from parishioners whom you know are "harmless" or "that's just the way he is" or "he just doesn't understand what he is saying." Of course, none of these reactions helps considerably, and they can easily morph into excuses for behavior and comments that are, in the end, inexcusable. At the same time, if you imagine a future with this person, how you respond will determine what that future relationship looks like. Your comment will not only be that which addresses the present but also that which puts a stamp on the future. How you respond to instances of sexism will result in consequences for your relationships—the relationship not only with the individual who commented, but also potentially with those who heard the comment and your response because these incidents tend to happen in more public settings where they are harder to call out. This does not mean that we do not respond so as not to risk a change in a relationship. It means that we are fully aware that the relationship has the potential to change. How you handle the situation determines, in part, the future of the relationship, but it is also true that the change can be a good one. Calling out the sexism has the potential actually to end well.

The most difficult reality when it comes to negotiating an instance of sexism is when there is a past and a present, but the future is no longer possible because of the comment that has been made. The demise of the future relationship can be solidified by your own silence where only you know and have determined that the relationship has changed. Of course, the other person will suspect something at some point and will either ask you what has happened or will also stay silent. The condition of the relationship can also be addressed in your response to the situation if you include an explanation for why a future for this relationship is no longer possible. In either case, this is a cause for grief. A recognition that grief comes with sexism is important to consider. Yes, there is justified anger when it comes to sexism, but there is also cause for deep sadness. Sexism not only has an effect on you, but also has an effect on the one who maintains it, as well as on the relationship between the two of you. It is necessary, then, to give yourself time and space to process this grief. It is a grief that is the consequence of a reality that could be better, that should be better, but that is so integrated into the matrix of our societies, and therefore, our churches, that curing it is much more difficult.

The truth about sexism is that it does not only exist in one-on-one occurrences, but is more often than not embedded deeply in an institution and its systems, including the church. The "church" includes an individual church on its own, the governing systems that organize the denomination, and the educational institutions connected to the denomination. At its core, the institutional church, along with most institutions connected to the church, is sexist because it is still embedded in, and beholden to, patriarchy. In many respects, it is not in the church's short-term best interest to out and oust sexism because there are still too many people who benefit from it and not enough people in power who have been the victims of it. Until this percentage changes, the church will continue to participate in sexism, either consciously or subconsciously, and it is much more difficult to call out sexism in an institution than it is in an individual. There will seem to be more at stake and more to lose. It will seem like it will take more energy and effort. And all of the above, unfortunately, is true. As a result, institutional sexism has a greater chance of survival than personal sexism because the risk appears greater in addressing it. It is, therefore, allowed to persist. Another challenge with institutional sexism is that it is frequently harder to see until you happen to be the one on whom it is perpetrated. It is very much like the larger and assumed contexts of our lives that shape our interpretation of our lives, but of which we are not fully aware.

Institutional sexism survives precisely because it is systemic. It is interwoven into the fabric of how the institution functions. It is inherent to how the institution makes its decisions, both large and small. In the end, institutional sexism, especially when it comes to the church, survives because we choose to mask it. We want to believe that the institution exists for the betterment of its employees and not to their detriment, especially the church. Yes, we know of corrupt institutions, but those are ones that lack a faith-based way of doing business.

What does institutional sexism look like? Will you know it when you see it? You will. It will be when a synod protects a longtime male pastor accused of sexual harassment by the young female seminary intern who "doesn't know any better" and blames her for naiveté. It will be when a church calls a female pastor but sets her up for failure. It will be when an institution has yet to adopt an official inclusive-language policy. It will be when a seminary continues to allow a male professor to use offensive, sexual language because he is teaching about the true confessions of the church, so that denominationalism trumps decency.

The church should be different. But what do we mean by church? This is part of the problem. The church itself seems to want to perpetuate its idyllic self: that it can exist and operate outside of or protected from the sin of the world. The church should be the prophetic voice that tells the truth about how its scripture and its structures have systemically and systematically shut out an entire group of people from its leadership based on gender. The truth about sexism in the church is that very truth. While we can certainly point to the leadership roles of women recorded in the Bible, the fact is that once the church started to become the church, the roles of women were cast within societal expectations. As discussed in KEY NUMBER ONE, we need only look at the depiction of women and women's roles in the "later writings" in the New Testament to see that as the church started to figure out it was here to stay, as it started organizing itself into an institution that could have staying power, it also had to figure out what to do with women. And in the latter part of the first century and into the second century, staying power meant structures reliant on a hierarchical and patriarchal ethos. So, the church did what any organizing body does when it finds itself surrounded by empire and partly reliant on that very empire for its survival—it adopted the empire's views of the world rather than God's. And therein lies the problem for the church. Once the church became the church, the church started to lose its way. This is not to argue that we would all be better off being the Thessalonians back in 51 CE. This is not to say that we can get back to some New Testament ideal, from the time before the church got too caught up in empire. There is no ideal church because, like the rest of the world, the church is made up of people, and sin wraps itself around the best of people and the best of intentions. One of the problems of the church is an odd claim that it actually is different from the rest of the world, or that it is immune to the sinfulness of the world around it. It acts as if it lives behind protective walls or surrounded by a moat, so that the evils of this world might not infiltrate the purity of the gospel. This claim to difference is what causes its inability to address its own sinfulness; its conviction that it is resistant to that which causes separation from God causes its own myopia.

This truth about the church is not what people want to hear and not what you want to hear as someone going into ministry. But it is a truth that needs to be heard in all of its fullness so that you are not yet another representative of the church who gets caught up in mutual back-patting and self-aggrandizement.

The church suffers from bipolarity between its origins and its survival techniques. And women have suffered for it. If the church were truthful about its theological claims, then we should have had women in major leadership roles from the beginning. If the church were honest about its own sin, it would have insisted that women be pastors long before large and successful companies finally allowed female CEOs. If the church were truly prophetic, women in ministry would not have experienced the resistance to their sense of call and to their desire to lead in the church. But only rarely is the church any of those things. How do we respond to this truth about the church? We could be demoralized and depressed. We could wonder if any of this is worth it. Or we could decide that the church is worth saving, not for the sake of the institution, but for the sake of how it might live into the full expression of God's vision of loving the world.

The fact is that fifty or so years of being allowed to have more leadership in the church cannot make up for almost two thousand years when women had few leadership roles in the church. The patriarchal and sexist systems within the church cannot possibly change overnight. We are just beginning. This is not to give the church an out or to excuse its behavior. Rather, it is to come from a place of generosity that moves to prophecy.

For example, even those churches that ordain women and that have been ordaining women have been painfully silent when it comes to institutional sexism in the church. The church overcame some forms of sexism by ordaining women, but that does not mean that it has dealt with its systemic sexism. An observable act alone does not address the issue that lies underneath. And the truth is that the church has done little to tackle the ways in which it continues to perpetuate sexism, not only within its own structures, but how it has failed in every way to be a prophetic voice in our world for the equality of women. The church, rather than being a voice out front in the movements toward equality for women, remains complacent and silent. The fact that women have had such challenging circumstances in their roles as women in ministry is demonstrative of the fact that the church thought that placing women in positions of leadership would be all that was necessary to address its inherent sexism.

CLOSING THOUGHTS

Your spark can become a flame and change everything.

—Unknown

Sin takes on many forms, but one of its forms is to destroy another person's soul. The sexism experienced as a woman in ministry has that potential. It has the ability to seep through our defenses so as to get at and undo the center of who we are. Sexism succeeds because we keep silent. We keep silent about its pervasiveness. We keep silent about the certainty of its intent to wound and even destroy. And to what extent do we keep silent so as to protect the church, the church that we are supposed to love, the church that is supposed to be the presence of God's grace in the world? Telling the truth about sexism is the surest strategy toward unraveling its power. We can do this.

EXERCISES AND QUESTIONS FOR REFLECTION

1. For one week, keep a sexism log of that which you observe and that which you experience. Catalog them, categorize them, and when they surface again, which they will, you will have a better sense of how to address them. Label the hidden meaning behind them. What's the underlying issue? What do these comments trigger for you?

2. Begin to imagine how and in what ways you will respond to sexist comments. Consider in what circumstances and for what reasons you will respond. What is most important to you in these interactions? What will be at stake for you?

3. Listen for the ways in which the media calls this out. For example, Stephen Colbert satirized, "Why does this gender inequality still persist, and how can we stop it? I don't have all the answers. And frankly, it's sexist of you to think I do just because I'm a man. C'mon! Besides, it's not my place to mansplain to you about the manstitutionalized manvantages built into Americman manciety. That would make me look like a real manhole."[17]

RESOURCES

http://www.dirtysexyministry.com.

Rebecca Chopp, *The Power to Speak* (Eugene, OR: Wipf and Stock, 1991).

Douglas Stone, Bruce Patton, and Sheila Heen, *Difficult Conversations: How to Discuss What Matters Most* (New York: Penguin Books, 2000).

KEY NUMBER FIVE

THE TRUTH ABOUT LEADERSHIP

For One Who Holds Power

May the gift of leadership awaken in you as a vocation,
Keep you mindful of the providence that calls you to serve.
As high over the mountains the eagle spreads its wings,
May your perspective be larger than the view from the foothills.
When the way is flat and dull in times of gray endurance,
May your imagination continue to evoke horizons.
When thirst burns in times of drought,
May you be blessed to find the wells.
May you have the wisdom to read time clearly
And know when the seed of change will flourish.
In your heart may there be a sanctuary
For the stillness where clarity is born.
May your work be infused with passion and creativity
And have the wisdom to balance compassion and challenge.
May your soul find the graciousness
To rise above the fester of small mediocrities.
May your power never become a shell
Wherein your heart would silently atrophy.
May you welcome your own vulnerability
As the ground where healing and truth join.
May integrity of soul be your first ideal.
The source that will guide and bless your work.
—John O'Donahue

INTRODUCTION

*The important thing is this: to be able at any moment to sacrifice what we are
for what we could become.*

—*Charles DuBois*

KEY NUMBER FIVE for unlocking your power as a woman in ministry is acknowledging that the leadership traits women possess, or the ones that they strive to develop, are not necessarily any different from those of men, nor are they any more or less effective. They are just perceived and described differently.

Any given list of ideal leadership characteristics will be desired by many a leader regardless of gender. The important thing is to know *who* you are as a leader. Notice the pronoun in that last sentence: *who* you are, not *what* you are. The central premise of this book is truth-telling, and you need to know your own truth about how you lead.

The first thing to recognize when it comes to leadership as a woman in ministry is that you are a leader. People will say you are a natural leader, but what does that really mean? While this may seem an obvious point, it is the obvious that often gets overlooked when it comes to women in ministry. This starting point, that you are a leader, is important because it affirms what is already true, not what you need to prove. You are already perceived as, and assumed to be, a leader in ministry. You have been called into this role because this is what people see you in, this is what you know about yourself, and this is one reason why you have entered into this particular vocation. Embracing this truth, embodying this truth on the front end of your ministry, is essential. You then move into your role with confidence and certainty, which go a long way when it comes to the efficacy of your power.

That you are a leader means that your position, albeit with all of the challenges named in this book, is already established. Your position does not need to be proven. Your leadership does not need justification. Your status does not need to be validated. That you are called to this station and title means that your leadership is already a given.

Where the leadership of women in ministry is less effective is when women reason that the first months of ministry need to be about attesting to the validity of their leadership. Rather than express what kind of leader they are, women tend to think they need to substantiate themselves as leaders, to provide evidence that rationalizes, excuses, and vindicates their position as a leader. As a result, the leadership stance is one of defense of their leadership, rather than one of demonstration of their identity as a leader. This defensive attitude will get interpreted in ways that are less than favorable and will undermine your position. This apologetic can be translated as a lack of confidence and an uncertainty about yourself, your role, or even your call to ministry. The self-justification that is perceived in you can also be seen as dismissive—the sense that you know what leadership is all about, that you have all the answers and are here to share them, regardless of your new context.

Important, therefore, is to do intentional leadership work prior to beginning your position in a church. As a result, you will know who you are as a leader, be able to articulate that truth, and be able to display, rather than defend, the core of your leadership skills and strengths.

You may desire certain leadership skills that are simply not authentic to who you are. Of course, there may be characteristics that you want to develop, but in the end, if they are counterintuitive to who you are, they will more likely be questioned or critiqued. This chapter leads with discussion about how certain leadership traits in women are perceived. You have to know the truth about these perceptions so as lay claim to those traits that you deem critical to who you are. This discussion is followed by a list of traits, so that you can begin to think about what is most important to you and what resonates with you as well as begin to plan for the practical ways to develop your own leadership goals and characteristics you want to nurture.

Why a whole chapter on leadership in a book on women in ministry? It is impossible to overstate how critical this chapter is for unlocking your power as a woman in ministry. You are a leader, yet you will likely embody leadership in a way that few have yet witnessed or experienced. You have the choice to adopt unthinkingly the leadership style of your predecessors, church context, ecclesial expectations, and denominational anticipations. Or, you could be you, and be the particular leader God has called you to be.

It is also essential to imagine how biblical and theological premises inform your understandings of leadership, and speak to who you know yourself to be as a leader. Again, it is not possible, in the scope of this book, to list all of the leadership characteristics present in the biblical witness, or to do an analysis of the various leaders, both good and bad, in the Bible. But it remains important to ask where and how you see traits of leadership resonating or intersecting with biblical traits. Are there leadership traits that are presented in the Bible that are worth thinking about for how you will choose to do ministry? What difference will a biblical imagination of leadership make for how you might go about creating your vision for what kind of leader you want to be?

BIBLICAL AND THEOLOGICAL LEADERSHIP

Modern-day perceptions of and taxonomies for leadership are foreign to the biblical writers. The authors are working with rather traditional views of leadership, particularly those construed by patriarchy. We could, then, dismiss the Bible as an antiquated and outdated resource for our imagination about leadership. Yet, in doing so, we would run the risk of reducing our imaginings about leadership in the church to the confines of secularism alone. There has to be a biblical and theological imagination for what it means to be a leader in the church; otherwise there is nothing that distinguishes a leader in the church from any other kind of leader. Perhaps you think there is no need for this distinction, that there is much to be gained from the leadership traits found in politics, businesses, governments, and other institutions. Certainly, the discovery of your own style of leadership, what is important to you as a leader, should draw from numerous sources and a variety of representations. You will be a better leader the more you observe, study, and discern the leadership characteristics of others—what works and what does not work, what resonates with you and what repulses you, what you want to strive for and what you determine are not your strengths.

At the same time, you are called to be a leader *in the church*, you are a woman *in ministry*, and the church and its witnesses should have some bearing on how you lead. Furthermore, those whom you lead are looking to how the church matters for their lives, what kind of difference it might make for how they live in the world. If what they see in you as a leader is the same as what they observe in leaders in the rest of their world, what reasons do they have for allowing the church to shape their own capacity to lead for the sake of God's love for the world? To what extent, when you embody secular models of leadership alone, are you also then embodying patriarchy by default? We have to be able to embody leadership grounded distinctively in how God has chosen to work in the world. One of the gifts of the biblical witness is the potential for a different ethos entirely. We might even imagine this as prophetic leadership, leadership in the true sense of Old Testament prophecy.

The prophets of the Old Testament were not fortune-tellers. They were predictors of the future only insofar as that future could be surmised by the present situation. The prophets were truth-tellers. They named the truth of the current circumstances, most frequently the estranged conditions between God and God's people. In this sense, leaders in the church must be truth-tellers. We name the truth about our sin in its widest definition: separation from God. We name the truth about God's response to this separation: God's repeated attempts to remove that separation so as to be as close to us, as intimate with us, as possible. We name the truth of how we are to respond to God's love and embody a life of love for the sake of our neighbor.

In this sense, we have a very particularized leadership. The traits, skills, and characteristics that we choose to embrace, develop, and claim as our own need to originate from this sacred space and place of truth-telling.

At the same time, this claim provides a certain hermeneutic for the ways in which we might approach the Bible when it comes to viewing it as a resource for our leadership imagination. In other words, rather than peruse the Bible for leadership traits here and there to adopt and adapt for ourselves, we look for stories in the Bible in which truth-telling happens, and how a leader becomes a leader because of that truth-telling. We look for stories in which new leaders are lifted up—not for demonstrated traits always known or expected—but because of a way of leading that comes from deep within the self, the self that has been loved, noticed, and celebrated by God. We look for stories where we feel a stirring in our own sense of who we are as leaders, that somehow, in some way, we have found a companion, a sister, a fellow disciple, someone we want to emulate, someone who should be remembered, someone whose traits we would like to embody in our own leadership.

In this sense, this chapter returns to the premises laid in out in chapter 1, on approaches to the Bible and biblical interpretation. This suggests an approach of generosity to scripture, even with its inherent patriarchy. This recommendation may not be embraced by all. Maybe your answer to being a leader in the church is to lead over and against the church, to lead as a critique of the church and the patriarchy from which it originated and that it perpetuates. If this is the case, however, you need to be clear about how to negotiate that stance in the practicality of your ministry. While it would be easy to shelve scripture as incapable of offering perceptions and examples of leadership from which we might craft our own leadership commitments, this dismissal comes with a price. We risk communicating to our parishioners that the Bible is good for some things in our lives but not for others; that in some cases it is relevant but in many cases it is not. Of course, this is a true statement on many levels. There is much that the Bible does not say, into which it does not speak, and for which it was never intended to have an opinion.

At the same time, our dismissal of the Bible as not relevant has as much inconsistency as our picking and choosing of texts. The harder task, therefore, is to go behind the cherry-picking, to name the motivations behind our choices. Once again, we need to revisit our concept of the authority of scripture and our views of the Bible. What we think the Bible is will, in part, determine when and how it shapes our imagination for how we choose to carry out our ministry.

If we determine that the Bible has little to tell us about leadership, particularly women in ministerial leadership because most, if not all, of the leaders are men, then our leadership as shaped by any biblical principles loses its mooring. At the same time, uncritical adoption of presented leaders, male or female, is not the better option, for it forces us to ignore the fact that the way leadership is presented in the Bible stems largely from values entrenched in patriarchy with which it is difficult, if not impossible, for women to connect. Unlocking the power of being a woman in ministry means being aware of this embedded perception of leadership and providing a critique of it, but also offering an alternative approach. At the same time, being a woman in ministry is calling out those moments in the Bible when that inherent patriarchy is being challenged by God, and in the case of the New Testament, by the words, work, and ministry of Jesus.

One example of this kind of approach to the Bible, of moving toward scripture with a hermeneutic of honesty and humility with regard to leadership and feminism, can be found in the story of Queen Vashti from the first chapter of Esther. Homiletician Carol Miles preached a sermon in the chapel at Luther Seminary in which she lifts up Queen Vashti not only as a model of leadership but also as one who offers a critique of it.[1] The first chapter of Esther sets the stage for the need of a new queen, which later in the story will be Queen Esther. King Ahasuerus is in power and rules the kingdom like any corrupt king would be expected to at the time. The synopsis is simple. The king is hosting a party in his palace, with the minions of his kingdom around him. The sumptuousness of the king's quarters is described in detail: golden goblets, cotton curtains, silver rings, marble pillars. In the words of Miles, what would really get this party started would be an appearance by the queen. The king sends servants to summon her and, Miles comments, "have her wear the black dress—no, make it the red one." In other words, in the eyes of the king, Vashti is nothing more than another goblet, another sign of his wealth and opulence.

But Vashti declines the king's invitation, knowing better than to enter the quarters of her drunk husband and hundreds of his inebriated friends. Vashti says "no." In saying "no," she names the truth about her husband and his leadership style: that he has objectified her, not only for his own sake, but publicly, in front of those who work for him. In saying "no," she stands up for her own truth, that she is worth more than the silverware and the linens and the gold and silver, all of which are signs of a kind of power and leadership that she chooses to reject. Vashti names that she has inherent worth regardless even of her title. In saying "no," she simultaneously gives up and claims leadership. There is no good outcome for her because of her decision. The conversation between the king and Memucan confirms that the result of her choice means the necessity of giving up her crown—they cannot allow all the other women in the kingdom to follow the lead of Queen Vashti. Queen Vashti gives up her position of power for the sake of her own personal power.

Her story also becomes a critique of the objectification and subservience of women. Memucan insists that if Vashti's behavior, her "disobedience," is allowed any lenience at all, well, then all the women of the kingdom could do the same (Esther 1:15-20). Memucan knows her power, names it, and crushes it. Acknowledging this truth names the patriarchy then and now because we cannot think that such things no longer happen in the world or in our churches. Power exercised by women is frequently power that is threatening and needs to be "taken care of." Yet, as Miles says in the closing line of her sermon, "They could take away her crown, but they could not take away her majesty." The truth about being a woman in ministry is the same. There will be attempts to undermine, usurp, or undo your leadership. There will be successes in those attempts. Yet while the position of your power may be jeopardized, or even jettisoned, the truth of your power can never be taken away.

Queen Vashti's character could easily be overlooked in favor of the maneuverings of the king, or as simply a plot movement to get to Esther. Instead, Miles gives Vashti her voice, and insists that her voice be heard. Vashti's voice is one that imparts for us an imagination for what leadership as a woman might look like. What are the leadership characteristics, then, that Vashti embodies for us? That true leadership comes from your true self. That leadership and power have a very interesting and complicated relationship. That leadership is as much about saying "no" as it is about saying "yes."

Unlocking the power of being a woman in ministry means engaging this kind of critical interpretation when it comes to scripture and leadership. It means approaching scripture with an imagination toward moments of ministry, hidden in the gaps and in between the lines of the biblical witness, from which we might learn. It means trusting that what is on the surface of biblical stories is not always the whole truth—much like life as a woman in ministry.

THE ETHOS OF LEADERSHIP

The greatest danger for most of us is not that our aim is too high and we miss it, but that it is too low and we reach it.

—Michelangelo

There is no end to resources about types and styles of leadership, books that review various leadership styles and their strengths and weaknesses, and definitive inventories that list the traits of "highly effective leaders." It is beyond the scope of this book to provide an exhaustive taxonomy of the different types, styles, and characteristics that seem to offer guarantees for what successful leadership should look like and be about. Rather, this chapter will present three fundamental paradigms into which these types, styles, and characteristics might be organized: leadership is autonomous, leadership is relational, and leadership is communal. Autonomous: it has to be about who you are. Relational: you are dependent on the other; you cannot do it all. Communal: you lead by example, aware of and responsible to a community that holds you accountable. All three need to be in play for leadership to be effective. When one overrides another, this is when leadership loses its purpose, potential, and power for good. The imbalance of these three critical features of leadership is perhaps the primary downfall of any person in leadership. Essential for leadership is the integration of your self, the other, and the world. While this taxonomy could likely be applied to anyone in a leadership position, there is more at stake for a woman in ministry in keeping these three elements of leadership in mind. Leadership as autonomous for a woman in ministry is critical because so much of women's roles in the church have been determined by outside perceptions and influences. The church has projected, and will continue to project, leadership traits that it has decided are acceptable for church leaders, but that are largely determined by male constructions of church leadership and leadership in general. If you do not have a stable, strong sense of who you are as a leader, the church will make sure that it shapes you into the mold with which it is most familiar, most comfortable (both of which remain male oriented), and causes the least theological and institutional friction.

Leadership as relational when it comes to being a woman in ministry is, likewise, crucial. If you are not aware of this necessity, you will feel utterly alone. And yet we will be told, time and again, that an inability to "go it alone" will demonstrate our inability to lead. This is one of those double-standard areas: dependence in men is courageous and demonstrates good leadership; in women, it is expected weakness.

For a woman in ministry, the relationships that you secure with other women in ministry will be your lifeline. If there are women out there who reject this truth, this need for support, who think that they can do it on their own, then they are women who do not recognize on whose shoulders they stand, and they are the ones who will burn out quickly, leaving a wake of resentment behind. Essential to unlocking your power as a woman in ministry is to feel the full weight and strength of the women who have gone before you, the pioneers, and in doing so, realize that you are one as well.

Leadership as communal for women in ministry takes on a completely different sense when we begin to realize that how we lead has a profound effect on those women and girls who are consistently overlooked by the church. The truth is that there are still not enough women in prominent leadership roles in the church with whom women and girls have contact. Furthermore, even if there are women in major roles in your denomination—if, for example, your bishop is a woman—you, as the minister, are still the woman with whom they have a personal relationship. You are inviting them to think about what it means to be a woman who has faith, who can think theologically, and who might want be called to a future in church leadership. This communal responsibility of being a woman in ministry is essential.

Leadership Is Autonomous

Anything may happen when womanhood has ceased to be a protected occupation.

—*Virginia Woolf,* A Room of One's Own

The autonomy of your leadership as a woman in ministry has to be completely, utterly, and convincingly grounded in an absolute trust in your inner authority, your truth. Your leadership has to be a reflection of yourself that is then acted out in your competency. Autonomy is taking responsibility for yourself and your life. The autonomy of your leadership will be revealed in your wisdom, integrity, vision, and courage. Autonomous leadership is embodied leadership: leadership that invests the self not for the sake of the self alone but for the sake of those who need to see what this kind of leadership looks like. People want to know what you stand for and in what you believe. At the heart of these claims is the fact that leadership has to be about credibility. If there is no believability in you, your leadership is automatically challenged.

Leadership is autonomous in that you must hold fast to the leadership characteristics that originate from your identity, authenticity, and truth. They are the characteristics that most resonate with who you are and with your core commitments. Yet, all too often, models of leadership are not about coming from your truth or from how you can lead authentically, but rather seem determined to make sure that there is little left of your body and soul. Leadership-as-sacrifice is not the same as leadership-as-autonomous. Leadership-as-overextension is not the same as leadership-as-individuality.

Crucial to unlocking your power as a woman in ministry is establishing your own list of what is essential to you as a leader. For example, when students in the Women in Ministry course were asked what leadership characteristics they viewed as most important, they generated the following list:

Grounded in prayer
A visionary
Humble
Authentic
Adaptable
Maintains perspective
Willing to face the shadow side
Comfortable being herself
An open, slow listener
A slow actor
Collaborator
Forgiving
Willing to ask for forgiveness
Open to the other
Fearfully fearless
Rooted in a theology of the death and resurrection
Self-aware of strengths, weaknesses, wounds
Vulnerable
Recognizes humanity in herself and others
Knows people and accepts who they are and what they need
Organized
Fosters relationships
Calm, levelheaded
Grounded in scripture
Relevant and inspiring
Risk-taking

While your list will certainly differ, the critical aspect of this exercise is that the first trait you articulate, or the first one to which you are drawn immediately, is likely that which resonates with you most deeply. Why? Unlocking your power as a woman in ministry cannot resort to taking on aspects of leadership that others think you should have. What is central to who you are as a leader should emanate from your very soul. What is the first trait, the first characteristic that comes to your mind? And then, ask yourself, why this one? It is not enough to make an objective list of traits. These traits have to be connected to your very personhood. They are performative manifestations of your truth. No one's list should be the same. Nothing is gained by identical traits. You should know your traits and be able both to articulate them and embody them. This is about personal and professional integrity. In that act of communication and incarnated truth is power.

The following quote summarizes autonomous leadership well: "She fell from their graces into her truth."[2] It will seem that there is no end to expected graces—that is, favors for the pleasing of others—when it comes to ministry in the church. The graces that assume that the bigger the church, the better. The graces that expect programming without proclamation. The graces that demand you be the "Jane-of-all-trades." The graces that insist you be the best preacher ever (whatever that means). The graces that demand that you be the all-knowing expert about the Bible, the pastoral care presence who always knows what to say, the minister who can pull a church history fact out of nowhere, the number-crunching yet vision-producing CFO and the ultimate administrator/CEO at the same time. The graces that say you cannot talk about certain things from the pulpit. The graces that are not grace-filled at all.

When it comes to church leadership that is prophetic, tells the truth, and insists that we go about God's way and not the way of the world, graces seem rather lackluster, and in fact, are not a requirement at all. In other words, when it comes to whom God chooses to lead God's church or how God will go about grace (from which we cannot really ever fall), obligation, indebtedness, and beholdenness are not characteristics of emboldened leadership. When we are too concerned about graces in our leadership, proper or otherwise, we lose sight of the necessity of risk, which will mean putting how you choose to lead on the line. Falling from human graces is an essential part of being a leader. Because once you start going down the road by which the gospel is about graces and not about grace, you know you are in trouble—big trouble. The essential character of God's kingdom is grace—true grace. Graces keep you at bay. Graces dismiss those who need grace the most. Graces ignore the truth. God is not about *graces* but about *grace*. So goes the church. So go those of us who are called to proclaim God's love. Grace tends to fall easily into graces, which is why as a leader you need to know the difference.

As the quote above indicates, there is much you give up when you fall into your truth and then live into your truth, out of your truth, and from your truth. As a leader, all of this is then readily viewed, out in the open for all to see. You cannot lead from your truth and then imagine a position of leadership that administrates without notice. The church desperately needs leaders who are willing to take chances, to take risks, leaders who anticipate resistance and challenge rather than avoiding or deflecting opposition and cross-examination. This is not leadership that seeks to be confrontational at every turn, but it is leadership that realizes that confrontation can also be a signal of growth and new life. It is, however, in that moment when we start sensing pushback that the grace of ministry starts slipping into the graces to which ministry can easily default. We feel discomfort, we intuit the questions, and then we begin to wonder if we are doing the right thing. Our trust in ourselves, in who we are, starts to wane and the voices of others get louder, so much so that the autonomy of leadership collapses into codependent management.

One imperative aspect of being in ministry and leading from your truth is anticipating that your relationships will undergo some significant modifications. Your relationships will change because you have decided that your calling in life is to serve the church. This calling seems worthy and uplifting when you are surrounded by others who do the same, or by those whom you serve. Yet, being in ministry is rather less commendable when you try to explain to those who have nothing to do with church what it is that you do. Your call to ministry will also alter the relationships with those closest to you. Ministry is a profoundly provocative profession to most. Even friends and relatives will have questions. They will laud your sacrifice but find your loyalty to God and church suspicious. They will wonder how to act around you now that you are a "church person," and they will self-censor behavior, language, and conversation to a level that they deem would be acceptable in church. They will start to question their own morality and what you now think of them. For some, the fact that what you do causes their own self-reflection and vocational deliberation will be too much for them to bear, and the relationship will end.

In other words, being in ministry means that how you negotiate life will change. It also means that you can no longer live toward others' expectations because those expectations are ending—both those placed on yourself and those placed on you by so many others. If you choose to lead by preserving graces—whether they be ecclesial, institutional, synodical, denominational, personal, or professional—there is much you will have to give up. Sometimes this choice needs to be made, but you need to know your motivations for doing so, and consider the consequences for your own self as a leader. You have to know what's at stake on both ends, whether it be graces or truth. Each side insists on much. And while it is not an either/or situation necessarily, one will most certainly affect the other.

Leading from the truth of the gospel means being willing to fall from graces—many of them. So many, in fact, that you would be inclined to think that graces and grace are the same thing. It is so easy to blur the lines between the grace we know and the grace we think we need to earn, need to secure, and need to prove. To fall from graces, all of their graces, means taking chances. It means bringing about the kingdom no matter what others think. It means calling a thing what it is: sexism, racism, ageism; even denominationalism, ecclesialism. It means risk for the sake of life, because God gave up graces first when God decided to enter into humanity, when God decided to become flesh.

The opening of Mark's Gospel is a good reminder of the kind of God we serve: a God who seems rather uninterested in playing it safe. Mark starts us out in the wilderness with a God lacking in proper graces. Abruptly, and without proper preparation, God explodes into the world. Tearing apart the heavens is a rather undignified arrival (Mark 1:9-11). Graces, especially those associated with a deity, would assume pomp and circumstance. Graces would demand some sense of decorum and dignity. Graces would expect an entrance worthy of the God of Israel and representative of God's many and mighty acts. But ripping and tearing the firmament? Well, that's rather untidy, unsightly, and unbecoming of divinity. It is impossible to put back together again, which is, in fact, the very definition of grace. Grace, by definition, insists that what has been *cannot* still be. That rupture means radical reorientation, even resurrection. That life reigns over death. That love wins.

This is, in part, what you represent in the church—a rupture. Being a woman in ministry means that what once was cannot still be. There is a tear in the managerial firmament of the church that cannot be mended, though many will want to try. Women in ministry still represent a disruption in the system, a breaking in of the truth that some do not want to believe: that we, too, are made in the image of God. This is, in part, why your leadership needs to be comfortable with disturbance; why it must even seek to disrupt, not for the sake of disorder, but for the sake of God's commitment to change. God changed God's very self, from deity into divinity in human form. Given this theological claim, it is hard to imagine and even comply with leadership in the church that stands behind, even hides behind, the graces that are complacency, conformity, and service to the status quo.

Given this God, we should anticipate at every turn that graces matter little. That graces are meant to be challenged, even shattered. That graces, especially if they are put in place to exclude, predetermine, judge, reject, justify hate, perpetuate ignorance, or to preserve systems by which we can continue to ignore our brokenness, are no reflections of grace at all. Our God does not seem to care much about graces. Our God is not confined to graces. Our God actually needs, desperately, our upending of graces, especially when they prevent God, in any way, shape, or form, from doing what God does best—giving life.

In this sense, your leadership life matters, and matters deeply, to God. Your experience of life in ministry will be truncated, diminished, even extinguished if you do not lead from your truth. When your truth starts to wane, people will start to see where they can take advantage of you. They will sense your weakness and insert themselves into your leadership for their own gain and power. It is in these moments that you will feel yourself begin to give in and give up, to sense that it would be easier to let go than to continue to be strong, and to feel that you just cannot keep at the hard work of being you any longer. This is when you realize fully that leadership cannot be only autonomous, although many leaders operate as if this were the case. Leadership by autonomy alone quickly dissolves into a self-hegemony. Relationships, perhaps once solid, dissolve because there is no perceived need for another. Autonomous leadership on its own will not want others around because relationship signals dependence. Furthermore, autonomous leadership eventually eschews relationships entirely because in relationship there must be accountability and the potential for criticism. Leadership that is solely autonomous will also retreat from community. There is no communal interaction because there is no concern for or attention to the community. The community is deemed unnecessary to the vision that is to be carried out; disengagement with the community is thus justified. These are the leaders that just "do their own thing," regardless of the resulting effects on the community itself. The various manifestations of autonomous leadership gone awry can be viewed on a spectrum: from someone who does not seem to care what others think to full-blown narcissism. Essential for effective leadership, therefore, is the awareness of the relational and communal elements of leadership, alongside a healthy, balanced autonomy.

Leadership Is Relational

I felt it shelter to speak to you.

—*Emily Dickinson*

Keep integrated, resist pulling apart. Have friends tell you when they see pieces of you drifting away.

—*Emilie Townes*

Leadership as relational is meant to consider the ways in which leadership relies on and happens within the context of relationship between you and another person. You simply cannot do this alone, and there are no rewards for doing so. You need to find the persons in whom your deepest trust might reside. Those persons with whom you can share all of the struggles of ministry but who will also come alongside you and speak the truth when they see your truth being compromised, replaced, or overshadowed. Leadership has to be relational because you need people around you who will remind you that what you do must come, first and foremost, from who you are; that you are not simply accomplishing tasks, working through a "to do" list.

Leadership has to be relational both when you feel your autonomy at risk, and when your autonomy starts to take over. Relational leadership is diagnostic leadership because it puts others in place to keep us in check. Relational leadership is honest leadership. It is honest about when you are not tending to the necessity of relationship, when you have become too caught up in your own causes to see that how you lead affects others, and when you think you can do it all on your own, no help necessary. Relational leadership is essential because many of us do not speak up for the things we need, the things owed us, the things that matter, or the things promised to us. We do not speak up because we do not believe anyone will listen, or that anything will change. So we stay silent: for ourselves, for others, in shame, in guilt, hoping that someone else will say something, speak up, stand up for justice, work against discrimination, reject false claims about God, and free us from theologies that judge. We hope that someone else will speak up for those abused, for those who have no voice. We hope that someone else will give voice to what we feel and know and want, that someone else will speak up for us. Someone will, but you have to have that someone around you who sees your need, your hope. The truth is that sometimes you do need someone to speak up and out for you. Relational leadership is confirmation of the courage to ask. It is very hard to ask for help and for what you need. But you will have to ask, so as not to lose yourself in your own autonomy and so as not to lose your autonomy. The courage to ask, however, is predicated on trust. Relational leadership means having others in your life that you trust deeply with your life and what makes your life matter.

As a result, the concept of leadership as relational brings up the role of mentors. The general idea of mentors works in some instances and for some reasons. It works when you are first starting out in ministry, and you are seeking out those persons whom you think you want to come alongside you, from whom you know you can learn, and in whom you see leadership traits that you want to experience as much as observe. At the same time, "mentor" may not be the role that you need or that is helpful for you. In the end, you need take to control of what this means for you. Leadership advice still tends toward the language of mentoring. If "mentor" is a term that works for you, by all means begin to imagine what it might look like in your context. For some, however, the idea of a "mentor," when it comes to leadership, can be rather one-sided. Success in leadership looks for those people who are mentors, those people who you want to be when you grow up, but the best mentors are those who realize the inherent reciprocity in any relationship. Mentors should anticipate that they will learn from you as much as you will from them, and that they will grow themselves because of this relationship with you. Mentoring cannot be one-sided. If it is a commitment, a relationship, then it has to exist in reciprocity and mutuality. The best leaders know that their leadership changes because of the fact that leadership is relational. They realize that who they are as leaders changes not only because of those who mentor them but also because of those who have asked them to be mentors. The best of leadership happens in relationship.

One other aspect about leadership as relational when it comes to women in ministry is the relationships that will be a given with the women and girls in your ministry setting. They will see in you what's possible for them. They will seek you out as someone with whom to explore their callings, if you let them. And therein lies the issue—if you let them; if you invite them; if your leadership style communicates that you are open and available to having the kinds of conversations that lead to the possibility for ministry. If they sense this in you—an openness, a willingness, even a desire for dialogue around a call to serve the church—anticipate a virtual tsunami at your office door. If they perceive you as someone to trust, someone who leads from who she is, and someone whose power comes from a deep sense of identity, authenticity, and autonomy, but who is also driven to the empowerment of others, then you will have a very difficult time figuring out how to schedule into your week the appointments with those who recognize that, want to be around that, and want to become that sort of a leader.

As a result, the concept of mentor, as a woman in ministry, demands a more nimble and refined understanding. You will need a mentor and you will be a mentor, but essential in this relationship is reciprocity. Mentoring is not simply giving advice, but recognizing where and how you bring out the potential in others, where and how you help someone gain skills and realize skills, where and how you see the situations in which people flourish, and where and how you are willing to name situations where people are not being allowed fully to express their gifts. There is power in these positions—the power to change people's lives. They will bring out the best in you, but in doing so, you will bring out the best in them: what they are called to be about in this time and in this space. Mentoring and mentors, therefore, cannot just be about what you learn, but what you learn in the process of this relationship. You will witness a way of power, a way of influence that has nothing to do with force and has everything to do with mutuality. Relationships in leadership that seem one-sided, governed by influence for the sake of individual gain, and intent on the means by which one benefits but not the other is really not mentorship.

As a result, if the term *mentor* seems conceptually difficult, it becomes essential when it comes to leadership as relationship to imagine the role of a mentor in a different way. The role of advocate in the truly biblical sense can be a positive image by which to think of essential relationships in leadership.

While the term *advocate* has legal connotations in our modern lexicon, the root of the biblical term opens up a host of possibilities for how women in ministry might embrace the persons closest to them as mentors. In the New Testament, the Gospel of John employs the term for the Holy Spirit. This is unique in the New Testament writings, as the Fourth Evangelist seeks to work out his own pneumatology as it makes sense with the person and ministry of Jesus Christ. For John, therefore, the Spirit is "another Advocate" (John 14:16 NRSV), that is, the presence of Christ when Christ will be absent because of his return to the Father after the ascension. This is important because the Spirit's work is the same as Christ's work, demonstrated in his ministry. What has Jesus shown while being the Word made flesh? What Jesus has revealed is what the Spirit then will do.

What does this have to do with mentors for women in ministry? It is an essential point of biblical imagination when it comes to picturing what advocacy actually means. In John, the Spirit is the *paraklētos*, the one who walks alongside you. The Spirit is the one who accompanies you. While the Spirit is the one who will indeed advocate for you (in the modern sense), it will depend on the situation. The Spirit's role in John depends on what the disciples need, and the Spirit recognizes that those needs will shift. This is what it means to be a mentor, one who is able to offer different things at different times and in different circumstances.

Another category by which to conceptualize leadership as relational is that of friendship. Why friendship? Because Jesus himself suggests this category to his disciples in the Gospel of John: "I don't call you servants any longer...Instead, I call you friends" (John 15:15). He is commending the disciples to the leadership of their community in his absence, and the category by which he imagines leadership in this context is that of friendship. This colors, of course, what it means to be friends with Jesus, and what it means to be friends with your fellow disciples. The concept of friendship in this case, however, has to be grounded in the conceptualization of friendship in the ancient world, rather than in our modern understandings.

Friendship in the Hellenistic social context was the second tier of relational obligations after family. Just as being in a family demanded certain requirements, so also did friendship, especially when familial relationships were severed and, in the case of the Gospel of John, severed because of theological and religious beliefs. True friends were those who had the other's "interests at heart" rather than having only in mind their own "betterment."[3] Friendship, therefore, was not just expressed in feelings but in accountability and obligation. One of the traits of friendship that Jesus displays with his disciples is "frank speech," which was how one was able to distinguish between someone who was simply a flatterer and someone who was a friend.[4] To take this idea of friendship into account when considering relational leadership recognizes the reciprocity and responsibility essential for healthy relationships.

Leadership as relational means imagining the success of your leadership as not only located in your autonomy, but also in those around you whom you trust to accompany you in your leadership role. They are the ones who will have to adapt and change, who you know will do likewise, and who will offer you different perspectives depending on your situation—not because they do not know who they are but because they know who you are, based in their own authenticity and speaking in full knowledge of yours as well. Relational leadership means that you have persons around you whom you trust and who not only have your back but will do anything and everything to make sure that your character, your sense of self, is never lost in how you lead—and at the same time, they are those who trust you to do likewise for them.

Leadership Is Communal

Kindness is in our power, even when fondness is not.

—*Samuel Johnson*

Leadership as a communal reality in ministry is important both for your own success as a leader and also for the health of the community that you lead. Leadership as communal means the constant realization of the public nature of leadership for the good of the whole. Your leadership not only shapes who you are, but also shapes the ethos of a gathered community. The very spirit of the congregation has the potential to be formed by who you are as a leader and how you choose to lead. When leadership is seen as communal, which should not be taken for granted, it assumes three essential modes of leadership: collaboration, collegiality, and hospitality.

When leadership is communal, it is inherently collaborative. If your starting point is that leadership exists within and because of community, then there is automatically collaboration. There is shared responsibility, which means that you have to give up some control and let some things go. The truth is, you will be seen as a model of leadership, something to take very seriously. You have massive influence, which is one way to construe power. You will make a difference (which is probably one reason you answered this call in the first place). But you will not have influence and you will not make a difference unless you take your authenticity and self-awareness as a leader seriously. One important reality of leadership is imitation: not only imitation of who you are, but also of how you lead. Not only will you have to believe in yourself, others will have to believe in you as well.

When leadership is understood as being communal, as well as autonomous and relational, then it cannot default to a way of leading that only thinks of the self or leads with a closed group of persons making all the decisions. Leadership as communal inevitably means dependency—on others to collaborate with in the tasks of leadership, but also of others on you to be the leader you were called to be. The question becomes why this element of leadership is important when leading communities of faith, or how this is different when it comes to ministry. Collaboration is critical in all leadership settings, regardless of the community being led. However, for communities of faith, collaboration should be viewed not only as a generally good thing to do, but specifically because it is a lens through which to see how discipleship works. Jesus counted on his disciples to make the kingdom happen. Community and collaboration are necessary for the sake of the potential for the reign of God to make a difference in our world.

Leadership that does not embody the essence of discipleship, this mutuality between leader and believer, is not leadership that belongs in the church. Leadership for its own gains, that does not picture the end result as being for the good of the community so that a community might thrive, is a kind of leadership that is counterintuitive to the leadership presented in the body of Christ. Leadership that is communal means that you look for collaboration in all moments of leadership. It means that you cannot imagine making decisions or setting out goals, purposes, and visions without gathering those around you whom you need to make those dreams come true. There was never a time when the disciples thought they were not part of something and their part mattered. There was never a time that Jesus led in such a way that his leadership could be successful without the help of his disciples.

The second aspect of leadership as communal is the importance of collegiality. You will likely start your ministry in an associate role, and it is even more likely that the senior minister will be male. Collegiality is critical when it comes to considering the communal nature of leadership. You are not only working together as fellow ministers, but your congregation is watching how you model leadership. How will what they see in you be different from what they witness in their lives? Will they see a spirit of collegiality that is grounded in the Spirit of God at work to bring about newness and change? The congregation will be able to see a lack of collegiality both in what you say to each other and in your silence.

This becomes a crucial aspect of communal leadership for both you and the persons with whom you work. As there is a strong likelihood that there will be a male/female leadership combination, how will you choose to be with each other? Who are the colleagues you can trust, and who are the ones you know will undermine your leadership? You cannot anticipate that simply working together elicits the kind of trust in which you can rely on others to have your best interests in mind. Rather, others have to earn your trust. They have to demonstrate to you that they indeed will have your back, that they will support you.

What does this look like in real life? It means that you and your colleagues do not display disagreement in front of your community. Leadership as communal means that you respect your community, what they need to see and what they do not need to see. You do not put your difficulties on public display, but deal with them privately. You work out your personal challenges with each other away from the potential of triangulating your congregation. If there have been disagreements with your colleague, they cannot be visible in a public setting. You can take the "high road" even if your colleague does not. At the same time, when public disagreement is inevitable and even necessary, you need to model working through disagreements and working together despite not always being 100 percent on the same page. This goes a long way in demonstrating that matters of faith are not always about consensus and uniformity and that the church should reflect diversity as much as what is experienced outside its walls. The challenge in this situation for women in ministry, however, is not getting thrown under the bus in the process. By being unwilling to call out the points of disparity in public and working with a colleague who uses that unwillingness to get his own way, women tend to be disempowered. While you have chosen to take the high road, your colleague has made the decision to one-up you. Whether the motivation is competition, embarrassment, or narcissism, the end result is that you have been stripped of your power so that he can maintain his own.

For as a woman in ministry, this aspect of leadership holds a number of challenges. It is in the moments where the communal aspect of leadership is forgotten that comments about you as a leader can have the most detrimental effects. That is, those moments when your male colleague makes a comment about your leadership that has less to do with you as a person and more to do with you as a woman. The same can be true for your council members, executive board, or any group that serves as the leading body of the congregation.

Leadership as communal means that you have a responsibility to your community to lead them, not to enmesh them in areas and decisions that end up eliciting their true loyalties or having them take sides in a debate. While the congregation will certainly favor one pastor or another for various reasons and at various times, they cannot be put in a position of having to choose to whom they will be beholden. This is also true for your challenges as a woman in ministry. Leadership as communal means that you will not entangle them in the issues that you have to face, so that they would then feel obligated to stand up for you, taking your side over and against another. The community you serve can certainly be brought along in your struggles, but it has to be done in such a way that they are not forced to follow one leader and not the other. This is a very, very fine line because the moment your male colleague makes a demeaning, sexist comment about you in a council meeting, for instance, your communal responsibility changes. The other women present are looking to you for leadership to call it out—and they should. While airing your dirty laundry in public is never the best option, once it is already out there—and not by your doing—the communal dynamics have changed. The communal aspect has been fractured in that moment by disrespect and disregard because the assumed and practiced mutuality and reciprocity has been set aside for the sake of another impulse.

Leadership as communal means a stance of hospitality. Why hospitality? Because hospitality is a hallmark of Christian community. Yet hospitality is a largely overlooked characteristic of leadership.

Hospitality was indispensable in the ancient world. There were few restaurants or hotels along one's journeys on the dusty roads of Palestine. Little travel was possible without the assumption and expectation of hospitality. In fact, there would hardly be a mission to the Gentiles without counting on the hospitality of the absolute other. We should not let two thousand years, and our taming of the gospel, justify the claim that hospitality is any less essential now.

Hospitality is not just having someone over for a nice meal. Hospitality is not just letting someone in for a spell. There's no such thing as "radical" hospitality or "genuine" hospitality. We like to add all kinds of adjectives to our hospitality practices as if to suggest that ours is better than others. At its heart, hospitality is, simply, radical. There is no other kind of hospitality. You either are or you aren't hospitable. If you welcome some and exclude others, do not pretend that you are hospitable.

Many of our conversations around hospitality in the church are rather one-sided. That is, we tend to talk about *our* hospitable nature, *our* hospitality as a spiritual gift, *our* "willingness" to extend hospitality, all the while patting ourselves on the back. Yet accepting and relying on hospitality is as much about hospitality as extending it. According to Jesus, discipleship demands dependence on hospitality (Mark 6:7-12), and this dependence is not just doing it, but more so, receiving and even needing it.

Needing hospitality requires vulnerability, letting go, giving up control, and easing into risk. It anticipates rejection at every turn and yet gives witness to God's love regardless. Your role as a leader, therefore, is both to extend hospitality and to receive it, showing others how to do the same. In part, learning to receive hospitality is an exercise in leadership self-care. People will want to provide hospitality to you, but we have a tendency to dismiss these offerings when our leadership style is weighted too heavily toward the autonomous. Nothing is gained by that rejection but some sort of "do-it-yourself" Christian ethos that is very hard to differentiate from the rest of the world. The rest of the world upholds that kind of leadership, that kind of identity, as admirable. Dependence is perceived as weakness. But in God's world, dependence is the way of discipleship. This will be very hard to negotiate, as the chapters before indicated, when it comes to the kinds of real needs you might have when maneuvering parish and home life. Can you yourself accept hospitality when your first reaction might be, "If I say yes, will they perceive my acquiescence as weakness? That I cannot do it myself? That I need help?" Admitting your own touch points about perceived needs is vital for embodying and communicating the meaning of hospitality as a leader. Your ability to receive hospitality will intimate the necessary convergence of autonomy, relationship, and community when it comes to effective and grace-oriented leadership in the church.

This kind of hospitality, this kind of showing of mercy, this kind of welcome, is Jesus's version of discipleship. As much as we claim its necessity and its importance as a mark of the church, we seem determined to communicate our inhospitable nature. We have extended and belabored conversations about who is welcome at the Lord's Table. We feign that welcome coordinators, name tags, and visitor cards in the pews suffice as genuine reception to the other. We justify biblical interpretations that result in hate, rather than in love. We persist in establishing systems and rules by which to secure our institutional, synodical, and denominational futures that come from places of entrenchment and fear, rather than openness and hope.

For women, we have long been at the other end of false hospitality— called on to provide coffee, cookies, and casseroles while rarely on the receiving end of hospitality from anyone except one another. While we were allowed in the church doors for some things, the list of acceptable places for and demonstrations of our service to God were limited. The treatment of women in the church reveals the fact that the church has been, and always will be, inclined toward a selective extension of hospitality. In part, what the church has yet to realize and embody fully is the mutuality of hospitality—that the practice of hospitality cannot be a one-sided affair. It is not just about letting people in, but imagining how you must change as a result. It is anticipating that you will be changed in this encounter, in this relationship.

As a result, churches calling a clergywoman for the first time might consider some hospitable suggestions, as if we are taking out the fine china for a fancy meal. One such list included the following: "Celebrate your new pastor; Treat her as your pastor first; Respect that she will bring unique gifts for ministry; Expect some resistance but avoid making very much of it; Avoid stereotyping and assumptions; [Note that] some things may not fit; Make sure there is a trusted feedback group; Avoid references to appearance; Pay attention to boundary issues; and the all purpose question to remember: 'would you honestly ask (say, criticize) this if the pastor were a man? If so, okay. If not, drop it.'"[5] While there is nothing inherently wrong with these lists, because they include helpful suggestions of things to remember, they come across as a checklist, rather than the basis for the deep reflection and intentionality around how a congregation must change and be changed with women in leadership.

Hospitality is more than a list of things to do when someone new enters your space. Hospitality is creating and inhabiting spaces for learning, conversation, and transformation. That hospitality is about creating space may also mean situations where someone is asked to leave the space for the sake of the community's health and ability to practice hospitality. It will be impossible to imagine and build up a hospitable place if certain individuals are allowed to ensure that it is actually not a hospitable place, either for those already there or for those who wish to enter. Hospitality is far more complicated than we tend to make it. Hospitality spaces also do not happen overnight. If you, however, start from a place of leadership that holds hospitality as a high priority, this will succeed in creating the patience for the time it takes to let hospitality take hold, both in you and in those you will serve in ministry.

True hospitality is far too vulnerable for most of us. This is the real rub of the story of the good Samaritan (Luke 10:25-37). Does the guy in the ditch really want help from the Samaritan, or would he rather die? The latter is the point. We would rather die than accept assistance from "those people." In fact, there will be people who refuse your extension of hospitality, who will gladly seek out other ministers and churches rather than have a "woman minister" marry, baptize, preside at communion, or offer commendation when you are dying.

You will have to take stock of the hospitality practiced by your parishioners and by your parish as a whole. You will have to take a good look at yourself. Where do you fall back into the so-called hospitality extended to you now that you are an insider? One helpful exercise when it comes to hospitality and ministry in the church is to do a ministry inventory at the end of each year. For example, if you preach regularly, take note of your sermons in general. Does your preaching practice hospitality? Address seriously your vocabulary, theology, images, illustrations, and stories on the basis of hospitality as a theological category. If it's a rare occurrence that your sermons offend (Mark 6:3), you may not be preaching the true hospitality of the gospel. If most of your sermons get only nods of acceptance and acquiescence, you may not be preaching the kind of hospitality that Jesus lived and insists on from his disciples. If most of your proclamation is palatable to your hometown, you may not be preaching hospitality at all but a watered-down version of welcoming the stranger. There is a lot at stake with leadership as hospitality. You are then practicing what you are hoping will be extended to you, and which has not been extended to you for a very long time.

Furthermore, there will be times in your ministry when you will desperately need hospitality. It will be hard to walk through doors that are just barely opened to you, and that have been locked for so many years because of your gender. You will want to downplay the importance of hospitality because it has been so significantly absent in the church when it comes to women and ministry, and you will think that if you bring it up, chances are that people will think this is all about you. You will have to let go of your excuses about discomfort and worthiness. Sometimes you will have to give up control and give in to what others want to do for you. If we want our churches to be welcoming and hospitable, then we have to demonstrate what that looks like in our leadership, and sometimes hospitality looks like removing the one person who is endangering the safety—physical, psychological, emotional, even theological—of the many.

This will be especially hard because you will want to be "strong," to show others that you do not need hospitality to "survive" in ministry. Instinctively, you will want to take a stance that suggests your power, independence, and autonomy. But it is in these times that people need to see your dependence so that they know they can be dependent on you.

This part of leadership as communal will not be easy and it will likely be uncomfortable. A theology of hospitality requires a reassessment of everything: practices, language, symbols, rituals, worship, confessions, and sacraments. To do this well will result in a church not simply "practicing" hospitality but being hospitable—and there is a difference. To find out what that difference looks like and feels like is worth every effort. Because to experience the kind of hospitality that Jesus has in mind is to experience the deep, wide, huge love of our God: the love of our God that shows mercy no matter what, the love of our God that became flesh so that the doors of the divine heart might be flung open to all.

LEADERSHIP PAST AND PRESENT

To exist is to change, to change is to mature, to mature is to go on creating oneself endlessly.

—*Henri Bergson*

Knowing your leadership style is essential so that you can differentiate it from others, especially those who have been in leadership roles before you in your potential call. The transitions in leadership are one of the most difficult challenges in ministry. These transitions are more difficult in ministry because the persons who have gone before have not simply been leading an institution or a business; they have been accompanying believers in major life moments: births, baptisms, confirmation, graduation, marriage, counseling, death. Regardless of who you are or how different you are, the human instinct tends toward comparison. When that difference goes from mostly ministry by males to ministry by females, the change that is already being felt becomes exacerbated. In that sense, you have the proverbial "two strikes against you," and it will require some thought as to how you might negotiate this reality. You can ignore it, you can make a big deal of it, or you can land somewhere in between. In the end, one means of negotiating the leadership of the past and your leadership in the present is to have a very clear sense of who you are as a leader and to be able not only to verbalize your leadership style, but also to embody it authentically. The leader that people experience you as must actually be who you are. The outside and the inside must match up. This is real. This is you being a whole person.

CLOSING THOUGHTS

How you embody what leadership is and what it looks like in your ministry is indispensable for unlocking your power as a woman in ministry. When people witness a kind of leadership that is authentic, they will be drawn to your power because they realize it is a power for the sake of truth—both your truth and the truth of the other. Leadership that knows the balance between autonomy and belonging is leadership that knows the giftedness of the self for the sake of the other. Healthy belonging is often the missing piece in leadership. This is belonging where you are safe and free to be who you are, safe to have your own thoughts, free to grow, aware of your personal power and expressing it, and able to ask for what you need. It is at the intersection of one's truth and one's need for belonging that we see leadership as companionship. Jesus knew this well. His leadership was one of accompaniment and encouragement, of advocacy and truth-telling, of deep purpose and love. We are called to be leaders in love, for love, and because of love.

EXERCISES AND QUESTIONS FOR REFLECTION

1. When you think of women in ministry, what leadership characteristics stand out as important?

2. What gifts for leadership have others identified in you? What gifts do you know you possess?

3. What positive models or examples of women in ministry have you been afforded?

4. What negative models of leadership have you experienced? In what ways were they negative?

5. Take two or three leadership profile tests, such as StrengthsFinder (http://www.strengthsfinder.com /home.aspx).

6. Take several personality tests: MMPI, Myers-Briggs, or Enneagram. While you may know your personality characteristics from one test, a different kind of test will illuminate your personality issues in ways that you had not considered before.

7. Develop a leadership plan. For best results, your leadership plan should include a list of goals, actions, and outcomes that will help you determine when you have achieved these goals and results, as well as a rough timeline for each goal to keep you accountable.

RESOURCES

Michael Gurian and Barbara Annis, *Leadership and the Sexes* (San Francisco: Jossey-Bass, 2008).

Tom Rath, *StrengthsFinder 2.0* (New York: Gallup, 2007).

Richard Rohr and Andreas Ebert, *The Enneagram: A Christian Perspective* (New York: Crossroad, 2013).

Sheryl Sandberg, *Lean In: Women, Work, and the Will to Lead* (New York: Knopf, 2013).

EPILOGUE

May God keep you safe until the word of your life is fully spoken.

—*Margaret Fuller*

THE HOPE for this book is that, in the end, it offers hope. But hope is hard to come by when the truth is not told. Truth-telling is difficult at first, even painful, as we noted and perhaps you even experienced in the process of reading this book. It is possible that much of this book has been more truth-telling than you ever wanted or perhaps not as much as you needed. But the act of telling the truth means that both sides of the truth can come to the surface, and then at least you know what is at stake on each end of the spectrum. The act of telling the truth means that what was hidden can now be seen. When issues emerge, when they are brought out so as to be seen, they then have a future. When we stuff the truth away, burying it in places to prolong its secrecy, the truth has the potential to cease to be truth or to be mistaken for something else. It becomes some sort of fabrication because it has been so long since the truth has been named. It turns into fantasy, lore, story-filled invention of what we think things are like, not what they actually are. The truth about the challenges you will face as a woman in ministry have to be brought into the light, so that you might turn your face to a future where you can speak your truth.

Some of the truth named here exposes the challenges you will face. But other aspects of the truth reveal the possibilities that are in store for you as you live into your call as a woman called by God to serve the church. The truth really does set you free. It frees you from the uncertainty of the unknown. It frees you from the fear of your own potential. It frees you for a calling in which you can embody fully who you are. It frees you for the embrace of others as they witness God's love acted out in your ministry. It frees you to experience true hope because true hope depends on truth.

This book could not be anything else than telling the truth because your calling as a woman in ministry cannot be affirmed with false hope. Truth-telling is its own form of equipping. It lifts you up from a place of honesty and forthrightness. It prepares you from a place of priorities and commitments. It encourages you by accompaniment in that which is difficult, not by pretending that difficulty will not happen, but by walking alongside and pointing out that the difficulty exists. One possible definition of hope is trust. Hope can be trust because the truth has been told.

In the introduction, we took seriously the term *power* that is used in the title of this book. Here in the epilogue we will imagine the meanings behind the metaphor of "unlocking" and the implications for what it means as women in ministry. We have unbolted, unlatched, unbarred, unfastened, opened, let loose, and released your power as a woman in ministry by telling the truth. In other words, the meaning behind "unlock" in the title of this book is, fundamentally, to set free. Unlocking your power as a woman in ministry is to be set free from once-locked doors or from that which we kept hidden. In many respects, this has to do with an unlocking of or a reimagining of your past.

Where you come from matters. Your origins are those things upon which you draw in order to make sense of your present. Your origins might be those things for which you long and that have determined significant aspects of your identity. Often our origins are idealized or immortalized, and we think, "If we could only go back . . ." At the same time, where you come from may be a place to which you never want to return—you cannot and will not go back. Where you come from might be that which you spend your present trying to correct or to make up for. To what extent have your origins become your present attempts to right mistakes, recast perceived failure, or reinterpret what was truly beyond your control into something you could have fixed?

Part of the hope of this book, therefore, is not only to give you an imagination for your present and your future as a woman in ministry but also to realize the role and importance of your past in the shaping of your present and future. "The past cannot be changed, forgotten, edited, or erased. It can only be accepted," reads an anonymous quote. The invitation to tell the truth about the past that brings you to your present moment as a woman in ministry does not have as its intent to erase the past, rewrite its truth, or beg its forgiveness, but to see it for what it was, tell its truth, and lean into the possibility that it can tell a new truth for the sake of your future.

To "unlock" also can have the meaning of finding out about something that was secret or unknown. We have learned about the secrets that the church keeps. We have found out about the candid realities of being a woman in ministry and they have been exposed. But more importantly, you have learned some things about yourself that you may have tried to keep secret from yourself and from others. You found out aspects of who you are that had remained hidden for too long. You have discovered truths about yourself that perhaps you never knew.

There is one biblical story that best encapsulates what this book wants to be. It's the story of the Samaritan woman at the well in the fourth chapter of the Gospel of John (John 4:1-42). It is a story about what—and who—can get unlocked when the truth is told. When Jesus and his disciples are traveling from Jerusalem to Galilee, Jesus insists that it is necessary for them to go through Samaria, although even a brief glance at a map of Palestine in the first century will tell you that traveling through Samaria was not, in fact, necessary to get to Galilee. In fact, any Jew in his or her right mind would not have gone through Samaria, because Samaritans live in Samaria. The necessity of going through Samaria is not a geographical necessity, but a theological one: Jesus has to meet her, the woman at the well, because in meeting her he shows us what it truly means that God loves the world (John 3:16).

The disciples go off to the city to buy food, leaving Jesus alone at Jacob's well, where he meets the Samaritan woman. They have a conversation that has become rather typical in John up to this point. Jesus says things that are hard to understand and the misunderstanding of his conversation partner either leads to confusion, as with Nicodemus (John

3:9), or to a greater understanding of who Jesus is, as with the Samaritan woman at the well. The conversation between Jesus and the woman at the well progresses farther than the one between Jesus and Nicodemus. She does not dismiss Jesus's words like Nicodemus did ("How are these things possible?"). Instead, she recognizes, albeit in nascent form, that Jesus has something that she needs: "Sir, give me this water, so that I will never be thirsty and will never need to come here to draw water!" (John 4:15). Jesus sees, and seizes, the opportunity. Jesus then tells her the truth.

And while countless commentaries still condemn this woman for being a "five-time loser," "a tramp," and "an adulteress"—with the implication that it is a wonderful thing that Jesus forgives her for her unseemly ways—nothing of the sort is really in the story if you actually read it. Jesus's request to meet the woman's husband is an act of truth-telling. He tells her the truth of her marital plights, but not with the intention of exposing her sin or immorality, because it would not have been her fault that she had been married five times. Women had no marital rights in first-century Palestine. Either widowed or divorced, she had suffered the stigma of poor luck, the sins of her fathers, but worse, the abandonment of one likely divorced because she was barren. Unable to have children, she would have been rejected not only by her past husbands but by her community. Jesus names her current pain—likely a levirate marriage, living with her dead husband's brother. Jesus names the truth of what would have kept her in the shadows: the truth of her marginalization, rejection, objectification, and feelings of unworthiness. And it is in that moment of hearing her truth that she trusts. She hopes. She sees that Jesus might have answers, and in her questions and wonderings, Jesus reveals who he is— her God, in the flesh. "I AM," he says to her, the first one in the Gospel of John to whom he reveals the truth of himself. It is a moment of mutual truth-telling, and in that moment she sees who Jesus is and who she can be. She becomes a witness. She returns to her town, a model for what it means to be a witness in John's Gospel. She shares her experience and her encounter with Jesus and she invites her fellow townspeople to come and see, to come and have their own encounter with Jesus. And they do. And they abide. And they believe.

In that moment of truth-telling she becomes who Jesus knew she could be, who Jesus needed her to be: one who testifies to how God truly does love the world. In the act of truth-telling that was this book, I hope that you have come to realize who Jesus sees you to be and needs you to be. God's love for the world needs your witness and needs all of who you are to be that witness to this world that God loves.

Let's continue the conversation. Visit the official webpage for *SHE* at www.bethefirstdomino.com and join or like us on Facebook at Be The First Domino.

I will close with this benediction, that you may feel blessed to continue to unlock your power as a woman in ministry.

May the God of Eve teach you to dance.
May the God of Hagar bring you comfort in the desert.
May the God of Miriam bring companions to you when you struggle.
May the God of Deborah teach you courage for your battles.
May the Christ who knew Mary and Martha show you the way of balance.
May the Christ who healed the bent-over woman heal your pain.
May the Christ of Mary of Magdala send you out to proclaim your story.
In the name of Christ who is the memory, hope and authority of the future.[1]

NOTES

INTRODUCTION

1. Kaylin Haught, "God Says Yes to Me," in *The Palm of Your Hand* (Thomaston, ME: Tilbury House, 1995).

2. Eliza Buchakjian-Tweedy.

KEY NUMBER ONE

1. William P. Brown, ed., *Engaging Biblical Authority: Perspectives on the Bible as Scripture* (Louisville: Westminster John Knox, 2007), xv.

2. For a concise summary of interpretations of Galatians 3:28, see Carolyn Osiek, "Galatians," in *The Women's Bible Commentary*, eds. Carol A. Newsom, Sharon H. Ringe, and Jacqueline E. Lapsley, 3rd ed. (Louisville: Westminster John Knox, 2012), 572.

3. For this distinction between embedded and deliberative theology, see Howard W. Stone and James O. Duke, *How to Think Theologically*, 3rd ed. (Minneapolis: Augsburg Fortress, 2013).

4. Paul King Jewett, *The Ordination of Women: An Essay on the Office of Christian Ministry* (Grand Rapids: Eerdmans, 1980).

5. Lindsay Hardin Freeman, *Bible Women: All Their Words and Why They Matter* (Cincinnati: Forward Movement, 2014).

KEY NUMBER TWO

1. For further discussion, see Karoline M. Lewis, *John*, Fortress Biblical Preaching Commentaries (Minneapolis: Fortress, 2014).

2. Margaret Miles, *A Complex Delight: The Secularization of the Breast, 1350–1750* (Berkeley: University of California Press, 2008).

3. David Gibson, "Mary Breastfeeding Jesus: Christmas' Missing Icon," *Huffington Post*, December 11, 2012, http://www.huffingtonpost .com/2012/12/11/mary-breastfeeding-jesus_n_2274119.html.

4. Oxford dictionaries defines *cisgender* as "denoting or relating to someone whose sense of personal identity corresponds with the gender assigned to them at birth."

5. "Sexism Terminology," Gender and Sexuality Center, University of Texas, http://ddce.utexas.edu/genderandsexuality/wp-content /uploads/2012/10/Sexism.pdf.

6. "Sexism Terminology," Gender and Sexuality Center, University of Texas, http://ddce.utexas.edu/genderandsexuality/wp-content /uploads/2012/10/Sexism.pdf.

KEY NUMBER THREE

1. Patti Digh, *Life Is a Verb* (Guilford, CT: Globe Pequot Press, 2008), 138.

2. Claire Cain Miller, "Is the Professor Bossy or Brilliant? Much Depends on Gender," *New York Times*, February 7, 2015, http://www.ny times.com/2015/02/07/upshot/is-the-professor-bossy-or-brilliant-much -depends-on-gender.html?_r=0.

3. "A Man's a Boss, a Woman's Bossy," YouTube video, 1:01, posted by SocialVoice LLC, December 9, 2013, https://www.youtube.com /watch?v=B8gz-jxjCmg.

4. Tara Sophia Mohr, "8 Ways Women Undermine Themselves with Their Words," http://www.taramohr.com/8-ways-women-undermine -themselves-with-their-words/.

5. Ellen Petry Leanse, "Google and Apple Alum Says Using This Word Can Damage Your Credibility," *Business Insider*, June 25, 2015, http://www.businessinsider.com/former-google-exec-says-this-word-can -damage-your-credibility-2015-6?IR=T.

6. Sloane Crossley, "Why Women Apologize and Should Stop," *New York Times*, June 23, 2015, http://www.nytimes.com/2015/06/23 /opinion/when-an-apology-is-anything-but.html.

7. Ann Friedman, "Can We Just, Like, Get Over the Way Women Talk?" *The Cut* (blog), July 9, 2015, http://nymag.com/thecut/2015/07 /can-we-just-like-get-over-the-way-women-talk.html.

8. Julie Holland, "Hillary Clinton Is the Perfect Age to Be President," *Time*, April 3, 2015, http://time.com/3763552/hillary-clinton-age -president/.

9. Fred Craddock, *Overhearing the Gospel* (Nashville: Parthenon, 1992), 16.

KEY NUMBER FOUR

1. Jessica Bennett, "I'm Not Mad. That's Just My RBF," *New York Times*, August 1, 2015, http://www.nytimes.com/2015/08/02/fashion /im-not-mad-thats-just-my-resting-b-face.html.

2. U.S. Equal Employment Opportunity Commission, "The Truth about Sexism," accessed February 15, 2016, http://www.eeoc.gov/laws /types/sexual_harassment.cfm.

3. "What Is Rape Culture?" Women Against Violence Against Women Rape Crisis Center, http://www.wavaw.ca/what-is-rape-culture/.

4. Peter Glick and Susan T. Fiske, "An Ambivalent Alliance: Hostile and Benevolent Sexism as Complementary Justifications for Gender Inequality," *American Psychologist* 56, no. 2 (2001), http://bama.ua.edu/~sprentic/672%20Glick%20&%20Fiske%202001.pdf.

5. Melanie Tannebaum, "The Problem When Sexism Just Sounds So Darn Friendly…" *PsySociety* (blog) January 2012, http://blogs.scientificamerican.com/psysociety/benevolent-sexism/.

6. Derald Wing Sue, "Microaggressions: More Than Just Race," *Psychology Today*, November 17, 2010, https://www.psychologytoday.com/blog/microaggressions-in-everyday-life/201011/microaggressions-more-just-race.

7. Ibid.

8. Ibid.

9. Emily Meyer, "Pastoring While Female: One Pastor's Search for Equity and Respect," The Salt Collective, http://thesaltcollective.org/pastoring-female-one-pastors-search-equity-respect/.

10. Jessica Bennett, "How Not to Be 'Manterrupted' in Meetings," *Time*, January 14, 2015, http://time.com/3666135/sheryl-sandberg-talking-while-female-manterruptions/.

11. Ibid.

12. "Our Mission," Weisman Art Museum, accessed February 15, 2016, http://wam.umn.edu/about#our-mission.

13. http://hindsightisalways2020.net.

14. Lisa Bloom, "How to Talk to Little Girls," *Huffington Post*, June 22, 2011, http://www.huffingtonpost.com/lisa-bloom/how-to-talk-to-little-gir_b_882510.html.

15. Debuk, "Just Don't Do It," *language: a feminist guide* (blog), July 5, 2015, https://debuk.wordpress.com/2015/07/05/just-dont-do-it/.

16. Ibid.

17. Stephen Colbert, "Stephen Colbert Shares Why He Thinks Women Should Be in Charge of Everything," *Glamour*, August 13, 2015, http://

www.glamour.com/entertainment/2015/08/stephen-colbert-shares-why
-he-thinks-women-should-be-in-charge-of-everything.

KEY NUMBER FIVE

1. Carol Miles, *In the Company of Preachers: Preaching the Old Testament* (Luther Seminary, 2007).

2. Terri St. Cloud.

3. Gail O'Day, "Jesus as Friend in the Gospel of John," *Interpretation* 58, no. 2 (2004): 144–57.

4. Ibid., 147.

5. "Suggestions for Churches with a Clergywoman," Lewis Center for Church Leadership, 2015, http://www.churchleadership.com/pdfs/To ThePoint/ToThePoint-SuggestionsforChurcheswithaClergywoman.pdf.

EPILOGUE

1. "Worship to End Domestic Violence," Overcoming Violence: Churches Seeking Reconciliation and Peace, 2011, http://www.overcoming violence.org/en/resources/campaigns/women-against-violence/week -6-stories-from-around-the-/prayers.html.

CPSIA information can be obtained
at www.ICGtesting.com
Printed in the USA
LVOW01s0822150616

492612LV00003B/5/P